THE GARLIC COOKBOOK
Revised Edition

David DiResta

BRISTOL PUBLISHING ENTERPRISES
San Leandro, California

A nitty gritty® Cookbook

Printed in the United States of America.

ISBN: 1-55867-253-2

Cover design: Frank J. Paredes
Cover photography: John A. Benson
Food stylist: Susan De Vaty
Illustrations: James Balkovek

CONTENTS

GARLIC — FACTS AND FOLKLORE

This second edition of *The Garlic Cookbook* offers fresh new recipes for soups, fish, poultry and meats as well as a new vegetarian dish, and updated recipes throughout. Whether your attraction to garlic is for reasons of healthy eating or creative cuisine, exploring the limitless possibilities of cooking with garlic will be fun and satisfying.

THE STINKING ROSE

Never has there been a vegetable as varied in flavors and mysterious in folklore as the intriguing garlic bulb. Cultivated since ancient times for its cooking versatility and medicinal qualities, the garlic bulb continues to capture the imagination of creative cooks and diners just about everywhere. Since 1979, when the first garlic festival was held in Gilroy, California, also known as the garlic capital of the world, annual celebrations have cropped up in New York, Virginia, Arizona and Washington. Often referred to as "the scented pearl" or "the stinking rose," each year more and more garlic is being consumed. Farmers throughout the world are growing a vast number of garlic bulbs to fill the demand for this fascinating member of the lily family, which also includes onions, shallots, leeks and chives.

Garlic is harmonious with most herbs and spices, and complements meats, poultry, seafood and vegetables beautifully. Baked, sautéed, roasted, fried or raw, garlic is used in many cuisines, including Italian, Chinese, French, Greek and Middle Eastern.

GARLIC VARIETIES

Fresh garlic is found in several varieties.

The **white bulb** *(Allium sativum),* called American or California garlic, produces very intense cloves.

The **purple and rose bulbs** *(Allium sativum),* called Mexican or Italian garlic, also produce strong cloves.

The large, white **elephant garlic bulb** *(Allium ampeloprasum)* yields milder cloves than other varieties. An elephant garlic bulb can grow up to the size of an orange, with cloves weighing 1 ounce each.

Rocambole *(Allium sorodoprasum)* is a wild cousin of garlic, with over 450 species. Its cloves have a mild flavor. Rocambole grows in serpentine forms, primarily in Europe and Asia. It is called by many names, including top-setting, serpent, giant or French garlic. Rocambole is rarely commercially available in the United States.

Green garlic is young garlic before it begins to form cloves. It has a milder flavor, so more is usually needed. The tops can be thinly sliced and used as an excellent garnish for salads and cooked foods.

PURCHASING GARLIC

When purchasing garlic, be sure it is fresh and firm. I prefer to purchase non-packaged individual bulbs, thus avoiding the soft, spongy bulbs that have rotted and lost flavor. Avoid purchasing or using bulbs that are shriveled, yellow or moldy. They have a harsh taste.

Fresh garlic is far superior to dehydrated and processed forms, but there are occasions when fresh garlic is not available or does not mix well with other ingredients.

In most dishes, dehydrated minced garlic or garlic flakes should be reconstituted with liquid before using; however, they can be added "as is" to liquid-based dishes, such as sauces and soups.

Dehydrated garlic ground to a powder combines well with flour, breadcrumbs or spices and adds a nice flavor when sautéed with foods. One-eighth teaspoon dehydrated powder, minced garlic or garlic flakes, is equal to 1 fresh clove.

Garlic salt is about 90 percent salt and should be used in place of salt in a recipe. About ½ teaspoon garlic salt will substitute for 1 fresh clove.

To ensure freshness, purchase all forms of dehydrated garlic in tightly sealed jars and store them in a cool, dark area with your other spices. Garlic powder and garlic salt have a limited shelf life of approximately 2 to 3 months. When they are too old, they impart an "off" flavor.

Garlic extract and garlic juice come from garlic cloves squeezed through a press and separated from crushed garlic. These are intense and mix well with other ingredients.

Preminced or prechopped garlic preserved in liquid and sold at supermarkets in small jars is fairly close to fresh garlic and is a convenient time-saver.

HEALTH BENEFITS

It's fascinating that something so delicious could possibly be so good for you. Garlic's written history of medicinal uses is the largest and one of the oldest of any cultivated plant. It has a reputation as a purifying herb, used as an internal as well as an external bactericide (bacteria killer) and vermifuge (parasitic worm killer).

Among the many recent facts about health benefits associated with garlic is the astounding data from the medical study at the New York Medical College of Valhalla, New York, which released research that proves that eating as little as ½ to 1 clove of garlic a day will cut blood cholesterol by 9 percent. It was shown that garlic reduces LDL-cholesterol (the "bad" kind) and increases HDL-cholesterol (the "good" kind).

Garlic has been linked to significantly lower rates of cancer in populations in China and Italy.

Garlic has been used to treat ill babies and children by various cultures for centuries. Recently, it has been shown that allicin, the substance in garlic that gives it its strong flavor, is similar to a European drug used to expel mucus and has been shown to be effective against colds.

The Monell Chemical Senses Center in Philadelphia found that if mothers eat garlic at least 1 hour before breast feeding, it can help stimulate the baby's appetite. The study showed that the strong flavor and odor of garlic enticed the babies to nurse longer and consume more milk.

Garlic's pungent odor comes from diallyl disulfide, a sulfur compound that is activated by contact with oxygen. It is easily absorbed by the body and permeates the lung tissue. Laboratory studies have shown that the sulfur compounds in garlic have anti-coagulant (thinning) effects on the blood, preventing blood clots.

Raw garlic lingers in the body longer than cooked garlic. Antidotes for garlic breath include breath mints, parsley, fennel and chlorophyll tablets. These have limited effectiveness since garlic's odor is also released through the pores.

It is not completely clear how garlic bestows health benefits, and there is a question of whether some of garlic's beneficial effects are destroyed by heat or processing.

TIPS FOR PREPARING AND COOKING GARLIC

Cut garlic by hand with a high-carbon stainless steel knife (see page 11). This releases only a small amount of the oil. Food processors can unevenly smash the cloves, which gives up too much of the oil and causes a harsher flavor.

To mash garlic cloves, if you do not have a garlic press (see page 9), use the back of a knife or spoon against a cutting board, or use a mortar and pestle.

Rub cut cloves of garlic on a roast, and tuck whole cloves inside the meat before cooking, for a nice garlicky flavor. Rub cut cloves of garlic on bread (toasted or untoasted) and then spread lightly with olive oil.

Some schools of thought say to rub a salad bowl lightly with a cut clove of garlic. Others say that this is not a good idea if you are using a wooden bowl, as the garlic oils will eventually turn rancid.

A new technique from the Gilroy Garlic Festival for roasting garlic is to place unpeeled garlic bulbs in a covered heavy skillet over medium-high heat, turning as each side becomes charred. The whole process takes about 15 minutes.

Various cooking methods alter the flavor of garlic substantially. Slowly baking a bulb of garlic will lessen the garlic pungency to a soft and mellow, sweet-tasting flavor. Raw garlic, which can be overly powerful, should be added sparingly in very small pieces to cold salads, soups, pastas and hot crusty breads. Minced garlic or garlic squeezed through a press, added to the ingredients prior to baking or sautéing, will add a distinctive savory flavor and aroma to the dish. Garlic burns easily, however, and overly sautéed or burned garlic will be bitter and should be discarded.

BEWARE THE HAZARDS OF IMPROPER STORAGE

If stored properly, garlic should remain fresh for up to one month. Keep garlic in a cool, dry place, but not in the refrigerator. A well-vented ceramic pot creates the ideal environment to ensure freshness. Don't separate the cloves from the bulb or peel the garlic until you are ready to use it in the recipe. If a garlic bulb should start to sprout, it's still fine to consume. However, the flavor will not be as intense, so the quantity may have to be increased.

Garlic braids have offered a convenient and decorative method of storing garlic bulbs (and in some cultures, keeping evil spirits at bay) for centuries. Braid garlic by the stalks, removing bulbs one at a time, as needed.

Be careful to use proper canning methods when canning garlic. Improper canning can release the bacterium that causes botulism and can cause fatal food poisoning.

The Food and Drug Administration (FDA) has issued a warning to consumers that homemade mixes of garlic in oil, garlic in butter and garlic in margarine should be kept refrigerated. The FDA recommends that consumers use infused oil mixtures shortly after making them and that they refrigerate all oil mixtures and discard them immediately if they are suspected of being spoiled.

I recommend that you refrigerate infused oil mixtures such as *Raspberry Vinaigrette*, page 45, *Garlicky Vinaigrette*, page 46, *Tomato Garlic Vinaigrette*, page 47, and all other recipes that contain oil and garlic for *only two days.*

GARLIC FACTS AND FOLKLORE

- In Hunan province in China, some people eat more than 50 pounds of alliums a year, including garlic, onions, scallions and chives.[1]
- The Egyptian pharaohs gave garlic to the laborers who built the pyramids because it was said to prolong physical strength.
- Primarily due to its odor, garlic has historically been associated with the lower classes, and although up until the 20th century it was taboo for the elite to consume garlic, the peasantry viewed it as an all-purpose preventive medicine.
- In Sweden, superstitious farmers tied garlic around cows' necks to keep trolls from stealing the milk.
- In some religions, including sects of Christianity, Islam and Zen Buddhism, garlic's odor as it leaves the body is associated with the devil, evil spirits and uncleanliness.[2]
- In ancient Egypt, 15 pounds of garlic bought a healthy male slave.[3]
- Garlic was used as an antiseptic to treat wounded soldiers during World War I.

[1] Susan Belsinger and Carolyn Dille. *The Garlic Book* (Loveland, CO:Interweave Press, 19393), 12
[2] Belsinger and Dille. *The Garlic Book*, 11.
[3] Michael Castleman. *The Healing Herbs* (Emmaus, PA: Rodale Press, 1991), 177.

THE COOK'S TOOLS

garlic cellar/keeper: a covered container made of stoneware, terra cotta or porcelain. These storage pots provide the ideal environment for storing garlic. The small, back-to-back holes allow for just the right amount of light and ventilation to keep garlic fresh. Garlic cellars and keepers are available in a variety of shapes and sizes.

garlic baker: a unique, easy-to-use kitchen accessory designed specifically for baking garlic. Baked garlic has less pungency and a much sweeter, subtler flavor. Season the garlic before baking and add it to seafood, poultry, meats and pasta dishes, or simply spread it on crackers or hot crusty breads. Garlic bakers are available in several styles and can accommodate from 1 to 5 bulbs.

garlic press: a kitchen tool used to press a garlic clove through small holes, extracting pulp and juice. A top-quality garlic press is an indispensable kitchen tool. Don't waste money on an inexpensive model. Purchase a sturdy metal press with a high extrusion rate. Most good garlic presses don't require the cloves to be peeled and are easy to clean.

garlic slicer/shredder: a handy, innovative kitchen accessory that is ideal for cutting large quantities of garlic in uniform slices. It resembles a mandolin but is much smaller in size. Made with strong, sharp stainless steel blades, it has a well-designed holder for securing garlic cloves while protecting your fingers. The reversible blade is excellent for preparing fine shredded garlic.

garlic crusher/extruder: a see-through vertical garlic press with the added benefit of storing unused portions of garlic. To use, simply fill the cylinder with peeled garlic cloves. Twist the handle to release the amount of crushed garlic you need, and secure the cap on the bottom to store the remaining cloves. It stores the garlic odor-free and comes apart for easy cleaning.

garlic peeler: Place 1 garlic clove in the peeler basket. Press the handle tightly, and a peeled clove of garlic falls through the bottom. It's ideal for peeling large quantities of garlic in a short period of time. It is easy to use and well constructed.

A new product, not pictured, is a plastic cylinder into which you insert garlic cloves. Press down and roll the cylinder, and the peel is loosened.

crack-and-peel garlic opener: a mushroom-shaped hardwood gadget designed to crack open the skin on a clove of garlic. Just hold the comfortable handle in your palm to get a firm grip. Press down on 1 garlic clove, crack and remove the skin. Turn mushroom over and use the round side to crush herbs and spices in a small wooden bowl.

6- or 8-inch chef knife: an indispensable kitchen tool for slicing, chopping and mincing garlic. The side of the blade can be used for peeling the cloves. Just press the flat side of the knife against the clove to loosen the skin. I recommend a strong, high-carbon stainless steel blade with a comfortable handle.

odor remover: a small, 3-x-2-inch flat bar made from a metal alloy that completely washes away the garlic odor, which some people find offensive. Simply rub the bar over your hands under cool running water. The bar causes a reaction that releases the garlic oils from your skin. For best results, wash your hands as soon as possible. It also eliminates stubborn onion and fish odors.

APPETIZERS

BRUSCHETTA

This appetizer is good to eat hot or cold. Be sure to use extra virgin olive oil and fresh tomatoes for a spirited flavor. Substitute mozzarella cheese for the fontina.

6 slices wide country or Italian bread, 1 inch thick
1/3 cup extra virgin olive oil
4 cloves garlic, minced or pressed
2 cups diced tomatoes, 1/4-inch pieces
6 marinated artichoke hearts
1 cup grated fontina cheese
1/2 tsp. dried basil

Heat oven to 400°. Toast or grill both sides of bread. Combine olive oil and garlic in a small skillet and sauté over medium heat for 2 minutes. Generously brush one side of each slice of bread with garlic oil. Cover oiled bread with a layer of tomatoes. Top with artichoke hearts and cheese. Sprinkle with basil. Place on a baking sheet and bake for 10 minutes. Heat under the broiler for 2 minutes.

ROASTED GARLIC CALZONE

Serve as a main course with a glass of wine, or cut into small pieces and serve as an appetizer for a crowd. You can prepare the dough in a bread machine, food processor, heavy-duty mixer or by hand.

1 bulb garlic, roasted (see page 50)	½ tsp. salt
1 pkg. active dry yeast	2 tsp. dried basil
1 cup plus 1 tbs. warm water	3 tbs. olive oil
1 tbs. sugar	2 cloves garlic, minced or pressed
3¼ cups all-purpose flour	

Squeeze soft garlic from roasted cloves into a small bowl. Mash with a fork to form a paste and set aside.

To prepare dough: In a small bowl, dissolve yeast in water and add sugar. Set aside for 5 minutes. In a large bowl, combine flour, salt and basil. Mix well. Add yeast mixture, olive oil and minced garlic to flour mixture. Stir together to form a ball. Place dough on a floured surface and knead for 10 minutes. Place dough in a greased bowl. Cover with plastic wrap and allow to rise for 1½ hours in a draft-free area. Punch down dough and rest for 10 minutes.

FILLING

2 tbs. olive oil
1 cup sliced mushrooms
1 medium tomato, chopped
3 cups fresh spinach, firmly packed
$1/2$ cup shredded mozzarella cheese

$1/2$ cup shredded fontina cheese
2 tbs. chopped fresh basil
$1/8$ tsp. salt
$1/4$ tsp. freshly ground pepper

Heat oven to 500°. Heat 1 tbs. olive oil in a skillet and sauté mushrooms and tomato for 3 minutes. Add spinach and sauté for 2 to 3 minutes, or until spinach is wilted. Roll dough into a 15-inch circle. Brush half of dough with olive oil. Leaving a 1-inch border, spread roasted garlic paste evenly on oiled half of dough. Cover roasted garlic paste with a layer of mozzarella and fontina cheese. Cover cheese evenly with tomato-spinach mixture. Sprinkle fresh basil, salt and pepper on top of tomato-spinach mixture. Fold dough in half to evenly cover filling. Seal calzone by crimping edges of dough with your fingers. Carefully place calzone on a lightly oiled baking sheet. Brush top of calzone with olive oil. Bake for 20 minutes. Cool for 15 minutes before serving. Serve hot or cold.

VARIATION
Top the tomato-spinach mixture with slices of prosciutto before baking.

FRIED ARTICHOKE HEARTS

Servings: 4

Serve hot or cold as a tasty appetizer. Use unmarinated artichoke hearts for best results. For a variation, substitute 3-inch pieces of celery for the artichoke hearts.

1 can (14 oz.) unmarinated artichoke
  hearts
1/2 cup breadcrumbs
1 tbs. garlic powder
1 tbs. freshly grated Parmesan cheese

1/2 tsp. dried basil
1/2 tsp. dried parsley
1 tsp. freshly ground pepper
1/4 cup olive oil
1 egg, beaten

Place artichoke hearts in a strainer and drain liquid. Slice artichoke hearts lengthwise into pieces 1 inch wide, 1 1/2 inches long and 1/2 inch thick. In a shallow bowl, combine breadcrumbs, garlic powder, Parmesan cheese, basil, parsley and pepper. Mix thoroughly. Heat olive oil in a skillet. Dip each section of artichoke heart into egg and coat with breadcrumb mixture. Shake off excess. Sauté each piece for 2 to 3 minutes on each side, or until golden brown. Place on a paper towel-lined plate to absorb excess oil. Transfer to a serving plate.

GARLIC CHEESE SPREAD

Makes 12 ounces

Serve chilled as a dip or spread with fresh vegetables or crackers.

1 bulb garlic, roasted (see page 50)
4 oz. Gorgonzola cheese, cut into
   1-inch pieces

8 oz. cream cheese, softened
1 1/2 tsp. dried parsley
1 1/2 tsp. dried basil

Squeeze soft garlic from roasted cloves. Combine garlic and remaining ingredients with a food processor or blender and process into a creamy spread. Transfer to a serving bowl and refrigerate for at least 2 hours, until ready to serve.

GARLIC SALSA

Servings: 6-8

Serve with Garlic Pita Chips, page 21, or as a topping for baked poultry or fish.

6 cloves garlic, minced or pressed
1 can (1 lb. 12 oz.) crushed tomatoes
   in puree
1/4 cup chopped fresh cilantro

1/4 cup chopped scallions
1 tsp. fresh lime juice
2 tbs. chopped jalapeño peppers
1 tbs. chili powder

In a large bowl, combine all ingredients and mix well. Refrigerate for at least 2 hours.

HUMMUS

This version of the traditional Middle Eastern appetizer has a little zing. Try using a wooden lemon reamer to easily remove the juice and pulp from the lemons. Serve as a delicious dip with fresh pita bread slices or sliced carrots and other raw vegetables.

1 can (15 oz.) garbanzo beans, rinsed and drained
1/4 cup tahini (sesame seed paste)
2 tbs. water
1 tbs. olive oil
juice and pulp of 2 lemons, seeds removed
6 cloves garlic, pressed
1 tsp. chili powder
1/4 tsp. freshly ground pepper
1/8 tsp. salt
1/4 tsp. paprika

Combine all ingredients, except paprika, with a food processor. Process for 4 minutes, or until smooth. Scoop into a serving bowl and sprinkle with paprika. Refrigerate for 2 hours. Serve chilled.

CHEESY GARLIC BREADSTICKS

Serve these on your next antipasto or with a salad or pasta dish. If you prefer, use your bread machine, food processor or heavy-duty mixer to make the dough.

1 pkg. active dry yeast
1 cup plus 1 tbs. warm water
1 tbs. sugar
3¼ cups all-purpose flour
1 cup freshly grated Parmesan cheese,
   lightly packed

2 tsp. dried basil
½ tsp. salt
3 tbs. olive oil
2 cloves garlic, minced or pressed
2-3 tbs. cold water
1 tbs. garlic powder

In a small bowl, dissolve yeast in 1 cup warm water and add sugar. Set aside for 5 minutes. In a large bowl, combine flour, Parmesan cheese, basil and salt. Mix well. Add yeast mixture, olive oil and garlic and stir together to form a ball. Place dough on a floured surface and knead for 10 minutes. Place dough in a greased bowl. Cover with a towel or plastic wrap and let rise for 1½ hours in a draft-free area.

Heat oven to 400°. Punch down dough and let rest for 10 minutes. Divide dough into 24 equal pieces. Roll out each piece and shape into an 8- to 10-inch-long stick. Place breadsticks on cookie sheets sprayed with nonstick cooking spray. Brush top of each breadstick with cold water and sprinkle with garlic powder. Bake for 20 minutes. Cool on a wire rack. Serve hot or cold.

CRISPY GARLIC-FLAVORED CARROTS AND ZUCCHINI

Here's a new and exciting way to prepare carrots and zucchini. The fried garlic slices release a subtle garlic flavor in the oil, which is absorbed by the other vegetables. Serve vegetables together as an appetizer or mix into salads.

8 medium carrots
2 medium zucchini
8 cloves garlic
1 cup olive or vegetable oil

Cut carrots and zucchini lengthwise into long, thin $\frac{1}{16}$-inch slices. Cut garlic cloves into $\frac{1}{16}$-inch-flat slices. Heat oil in a deep skillet. Sauté carrot, zucchini and garlic slices for 2 to 3 minutes, or until edges turn slightly brown and crisp. Place on a paper towel-lined plate to drain. Cool and serve at room temperature.

GARLIC PITA CHIPS

Delicious and addictive. I enjoy these served with cold Garlic Salsa, *page 17, but they easily stand on their own and can be prepared a day in advance. Serve hot or cold as chips, or with a thin slice of Monterey Jack cheese.*

2 tbs. butter
1/2 cup olive oil
8 cloves garlic, pressed
6 loaves pita bread

Heat oven to 350°. Melt butter in a small saucepan. Add olive oil and garlic to melted butter and sauté over low heat for 10 minutes. Split open pita pockets and cut in half. Each pita will make 4 half-moon shapes. With rough side up, lay pita slices on a baking sheet. Brush entire surface with garlic mixture. Bake for 10 minutes. Place under the broiler for 1 minute, or until golden brown. Remove from oven and place on paper towels to absorb excess oil. Break into 2-inch pieces and serve in a large bowl or towel-lined wicker basket.

VARIATION
Sprinkle with dried basil or oregano before baking.

GARLIC-FLAVORED POPCORN

This is a dramatic twist to ordinary popcorn. It is simple to prepare and should be served immediately for maximum flavor.

3 tbs. butter
$\frac{1}{2}$ tsp. garlic powder
2 tbs. vegetable oil
$\frac{1}{2}$ cup high-quality popcorn kernels

Melt butter in a small saucepan. Add garlic powder and mix well. Heat oil in a $3\frac{1}{2}$- to $4\frac{1}{2}$-quart pot over medium-high heat for 20 seconds. Add popcorn kernels. Stir until all kernels are coated with oil. Cover pot. As soon as the first kernel pops, shake continuously until all kernels have popped. Remove from heat and empty popped kernels into a large bowl. Add melted garlic butter and toss.

VARIATION

For a special treat, flavor popped kernels with $\frac{3}{4}$ cup finely grated cheddar cheese and place in a preheated 325° oven for 6 minutes.

GARLIC BREAD

Garlic bread was probably invented in the United States during the era of Italian-American restaurants in the late 1940s. You can also use Italian bread.

1 loaf French bread, halved lengthwise $\frac{1}{2}$ cup butter
4 cloves garlic, cut in half

Place bread under the broiler and toast lightly, carefully watching to avoid burning. Remove bread from oven and quickly rub crusty surface with cut garlic. Butter bread. Serve immediately, or reheat in the oven for 3 to 5 minutes before serving.

GARLIC HERB BUTTER

Makes $\frac{1}{2}$ cup

Use for warm bread or rolls, or when cooking fish, lamb, vegetables or poultry. For an elegant touch, place the butter in the freezer for 20 minutes, and use a butter curler to scrape sculptured swirls.

$\frac{1}{2}$ cup butter or margarine, softened $\frac{1}{2}$ tsp. dried basil
2 cloves garlic, pressed $\frac{1}{2}$ tsp. dried thyme

Combine all ingredients in a food processor workbowl or blend together in a small bowl with a fork or spoon. Keep refrigerated or freeze for future use.

PIZZA CRUST AND TWO TOPPINGS

Servings: 6-8 each pizza

Choose from two flavorful toppings for this delicious crust: a traditional tomato sauce topping, or a spicy Southwest-style topping. Bread machines, food processors and heavy-duty mixers stand in for hand-kneading.

CRUST

1 pkg. active dry yeast
1 cup plus 1 tbs. warm water
1 tbs. sugar
3¼ cups all-purpose flour

½ tsp. salt
2 tsp. dried basil
3 tbs. olive oil
2 cloves garlic, minced or pressed

In a small bowl, dissolve yeast in water and add sugar. Set aside for 5 minutes. In a large bowl, combine flour, salt and basil and mix well. Add yeast mixture, olive oil and garlic and stir together to form a ball. Place dough on a floured surface and knead for 10 minutes. Place in a greased bowl, cover with plastic wrap and let rise for 1½ hours in a draft-free area.

Heat oven to 425°. Punch down dough and let rest for 10 minutes. Roll out dough to fit a 14-inch pizza pan or ceramic baking stone.

GARLIC-HERB PIZZA TOPPING

¾ cup tomato pizza sauce
1 tomato, thinly sliced
2 cloves garlic, thinly sliced
¾ cup shredded mozzarella cheese

1 cup shredded Monterey Jack cheese
1 tbs. freshly grated Parmesan cheese
1 tsp. dried oregano

Spoon tomato sauce evenly over dough, leaving a 1-inch border around outside edge. Top with tomato and garlic slices and cheeses. Sprinkle with oregano. Bake for 25 minutes.

TEX-MEX GARLIC PIZZA TOPPING

2 tbs. olive oil
¾ cup shredded mozzarella cheese
¾ cup shredded Monterey Jack cheese
¾ cup grated Parmesan cheese
6 cloves garlic, minced

1 tsp. dried red pepper flakes
2 tsp. dried jalapeño flakes or 4
   jalapeño peppers, seeded and finely
   chopped
½ tsp. chili powder

Brush dough with olive oil. Top with cheeses. Sprinkle with minced garlic, red pepper flakes, jalapeño flakes and chili powder. Bake for 25 to 30 minutes, or until cheese bubbles and is golden brown.

GARLIC AND HERB FOCACCIA

Servings: 8-12

This flavorful focaccia goes well with just about any dish. Use a food processor, heavy-duty mixer or bread machine, if desired.

1 pkg. active dry yeast
1 cup plus 1 tbs. warm water
1 tbs. sugar
3¼ cups all-purpose flour
½ tsp. salt

5 tbs. olive oil
2 cloves garlic, pressed
½ tsp. ground dried rosemary
½ tsp. dried basil

In a small bowl, dissolve yeast in water and add sugar. Set aside for 5 minutes. In a large bowl, combine flour and salt. Mix well. Add yeast mixture, 3 tbs. olive oil and garlic and stir together to form a ball. Place dough on a floured surface and knead for 10 minutes. Place dough in a greased bowl, cover with plastic wrap and let rise for 1½ hours in a draft-free area.

Heat oven to 400°. Punch down dough and let rest for 10 minutes. Roll out dough to fit an 8½-x-12-inch baking pan. Brush bottom and sides of pan with olive oil. Place dough in pan, pressing and stretching so it extends to all sides of pan. Pierce dough with a fork about every 2 to 3 inches and brush top with olive oil. Sprinkle with rosemary and basil. Bake for 25 minutes. Brush top with remaining olive oil and broil for 3 to 5 minutes, or until top is golden brown. Serve hot or at room temperature.

RIO RANCHERO SEAFOOD SALSA

Serve with Garlic Pita Chips, *page 21, as a topping for tacos or as a meal in itself — the fresh garlic and seafood come together beautifully for a spicy and nutritious meal.*

1 can (1 lb. 12 oz.) crushed tomato in puree
1 medium onion, finely chopped
6 cloves garlic, minced or pressed
2 tbs. chopped jalapeño peppers
1 tbs. chili powder
1 can (4.5 oz.) mild green chile peppers
1 tsp. finely chopped fresh cilantro
½ lb. cooked small shrimp, or large shrimp cut into bite-sized pieces
½ lb. cooked crabmeat, shredded into bite-sized pieces

In a large bowl, combine crushed tomato, onion, garlic, peppers, chili powder, chile peppers and cilantro. Mix thoroughly. Stir in shrimp and crabmeat. Cover bowl and refrigerate for at least 2 hours. Serve chilled.

ROASTED GARLIC PASTRY PUFFS

Serve these at your next party. They'll be a sure hit. The crust is delicious, the filling is incredible and the garlic flavor is mellow.

FILLING

2 bulbs garlic, roasted (see page 50)
1/4 cup butter
1/2 cup finely chopped celery
1 cup finely chopped onions
3 1/2 cups finely chopped mushrooms
1/2 tsp. dried thyme

PASTRY

1/4 cup butter, softened
3/4 cup shredded cheddar cheese
1/4 cup shredded Monterey Jack cheese
1 cup flour
2 tbs. water

To prepare filling: Separate roasted garlic cloves, peel and mash together to form a paste. Melt butter in a skillet. Add celery and onions. Sauté on medium heat for 5 minutes. Add garlic paste and sauté for 4 minutes. Add mushrooms and thyme; sauté for 6 minutes. Set aside to cool.

To prepare pastry: In a medium bowl, cream together butter and cheeses. Blend flour into mixture. Starting with 1 tbs., add water as needed to form dough.

Heat oven to 400°. Roll dough into thin sheets and cut into 4-x-4-inch squares. Place a teaspoon of filling on a corner, covering about half of the square, at an angle. Fold over other half of dough to form a triangle. Crimp edges to seal. Place pastry puffs on a nonstick or lightly greased cookie sheet. Bake for 20 minutes, or until golden brown. Cool and serve at room temperature.

ROASTED GARLIC AND BROCCOLI CHEESE SPREAD

The roasted garlic adds a rich and delicious flavor to the spread without any added fat. Make this ahead of time. It's a perfect dip for a casual party setting. Serve with crackers or fresh vegetables.

4 cloves garlic, roasted (see page 50)
$1/2$ lb. broccoli florets and stems
8 oz. cream cheese
2 tsp. chives

Remove skin or squeeze soft garlic from roasted cloves and set aside. Cook broccoli in a steamer for 3 to 4 minutes, or until bright green. Set aside to cool. In a food processor workbowl, combine broccoli, garlic, cream cheese and chives; process until mixture is smooth. Remove from workbowl and chill for $2 1/2$ hours.

GUACAMOLE

Serve with Garlic Pita Chips, *page 21, or raw vegetables, or as a salad topping. For a variation, mix in diced tomatoes, sliced olives or chopped hard-cooked eggs and serve as a sandwich spread.*

2 ripe avocados
1 can (4.5 oz.) green chile peppers, finely chopped
4 cloves garlic, minced or pressed
juice of 1 lime
1 medium onion, finely chopped
3 tbs. finely chopped fresh cilantro
1 tbs. finely chopped jalapeño peppers
1 tsp. chili powder
$1/8$ tsp. ground cumin
$1/8$ tsp. freshly ground pepper
$1/8$ tsp. salt

Peel avocados and remove pits; mash in a bowl with a fork until smooth but a little chunky. Combine with remaining ingredients, cover and refrigerate for 2 hours.

MARINATED MUSHROOMS

Always buy fresh mushrooms and use them within 3 days.

36 mushrooms
1 can (14.5 oz.) stewed tomatoes, chopped, with juice
1/2 cup dry sherry
1/3 cup olive oil
2 tbs. balsamic vinegar
1/4 tsp. freshly ground pepper
6 cloves garlic, minced or pressed
juice of 1/2 lemon
2 tsp. dried oregano

Clean mushrooms with a damp cloth or a mushroom brush with soft bristles. If you wash mushrooms, use cold water and drain on paper towels until dry. Combine remaining ingredients in a large bowl and mix thoroughly. Add mushrooms. Cover with a tight seal and place in the refrigerator for 1 to 2 days. Stir occasionally.

SOUPS AND SALADS

GARLIC ONION SOUP

Serve as a first course or as an accompaniment to a fresh salad or sandwich.

1 bulb garlic, roasted (see page 48)
3 tbs. butter
5 medium onions, thinly sliced
1 can (13¾ oz.) beef broth
7 cups water
4 beef bouillon cubes
1 tbs. Worcestershire sauce
Garlic Croutons, page 38

Squeeze roasted garlic from each clove and set aside. Melt butter in a skillet. Add onion slices and sauté over medium-low heat for 30 minutes. Do not cover skillet. In a large saucepan or stockpot, combine beef broth, water, bouillon cubes, Worcestershire sauce and roasted garlic. Simmer for 30 minutes. Remove broth mixture from heat and cool; pour into a food processor workbowl or blender container and puree. You may have to process this in two or three batches. Return pureed mixture to stockpot. Add sautéed onions and simmer for 30 minutes. Serve in individual soup bowls with *Garlic Croutons*.

CURRIED CHESTNUT SOUP

Servings: 6

You can use fresh chestnuts for roasting, available in the supermarkets from late October through December, or bottled and canned varieties, available year-round.

1 tbs. olive oil
1 1/2 cups chopped onion
2 cloves garlic, minced or pressed
1 3/4 tsp. curry powder
2 cups diced sweet potatoes
2 cups 2-inch green bean pieces
1 can (14.5 oz.) white kidney beans,
    rinsed and drained

5 cups chicken broth
2 cups water
1 1/2 cups chopped cooked chestnuts
1/2 tsp. dried basil
1/4 tsp. ground cumin
1 can (14.5 oz.) stewed tomatoes,
    drained and chopped
salt and pepper to taste

Heat oil in a large Dutch oven over medium heat. Add onions and sauté for 4 to 5 minutes. Add curry powder, garlic and sweet potatoes and sauté for 5 minutes. Add green beans, kidney beans, chicken broth and water and bring to a boil. Cover and simmer for 30 minutes or until sweet potatoes are tender. Transfer 4 cups of the soup to a blender container or food processor workbowl and puree until smooth. Return to Dutch oven; stir in stewed tomatoes, basil and cumin. Heat thoroughly and serve.

PUMPKIN SOUP

This low-fat recipe is surprisingly rich in flavor with a creamy texture. Full of the season's flavors, it's perfect on a chilly fall day.

2 tsp. butter
1 cup chopped onion
2 cloves garlic, pressed or minced
1/4 tsp. ground cumin
1/2 tsp. curry powder
1/4 tsp. ground nutmeg
3 tbs. flour

5 1/4 cups low-sodium chicken broth
1/4 tsp. salt
1 1/2 cups canned pumpkin puree
2 cups peeled, diced sweet potatoes
1/3 cup evaporated skim milk
fresh chive sprigs for garnish

Melt butter in a large stockpot over medium heat. Add onion and sauté for 3 minutes. Add garlic, cumin, curry and nutmeg and sauté for 1 minute. Stir in flour and sauté for 1 minute. Add broth, salt, pumpkin puree and diced sweet potato. Stir well and bring to a boil. Partially cover, reduce heat and simmer for 20 to 25 minutes or until sweet potatoes are tender, stirring occasionally. Remove from heat and cool for 10 to 15 minutes. Place mixture in a blender container or food processor workbowl and process until smooth. Return mixture to stockpot; add milk and stir well. Cook until thoroughly heated. Garnish with fresh chive sprigs if desired.

SAUSAGE SOUP WITH SPINACH AND LONG-GRAIN RICE

The sausage gives this soup a spicy kick. Serve it with a fresh garden salad and slices of crusty Italian country-style bread.

1 lb. hot Italian sausage, casing removed
1 tbs. olive oil
1 cup chopped onion
3 cloves garlic, crushed
9 cups chicken broth
½ cup canned diced tomatoes, with juice

3 tbs. tomato paste
1 tsp. dried oregano
1 tsp. dried basil
3 cups fresh baby spinach, torn into 2-3 inch pieces
2 cups cooked long-grain white rice
salt and pepper to taste
¼ cup freshly grated Parmesan cheese

Sauté sausage in a large stockpot over medium-high heat until cooked, about 10 minutes. Remove sausage from pot and discard drippings. Add olive oil to pot and heat. Add onion and sauté for 3 to 4 minutes or until translucent. Add garlic and sauté for 1 minute. Return sausage to pot. Add broth, tomatoes, tomato paste, oregano and basil. Simmer for 20 minutes. Add spinach and rice and continue to simmer until spinach is just wilted. Serve topped with Parmesan cheese.

TOMATO SLICES WITH BASIL AND GARLIC

Servings: 4-6

For this traditional Italian favorite, use only vine-ripened, fresh tomatoes. Serve as a salad or on a platter for a buffet.

6 medium tomatoes
1/4 head lettuce
2 cloves garlic, minced or pressed
2 tbs. minced fresh basil
1/2 tsp. freshly ground pepper
1/4 cup light extra virgin olive oil

Cut tomatoes into 1/4-inch slices. Line a platter or small individual plates with fresh lettuce. Arrange a layer of tomato slices on top of lettuce. Combine garlic, basil, pepper and olive oil and sprinkle over tomato slices. Refrigerate for 1 hour before serving.

CAESAR SALAD

A shallow wooden bowl made of hard rock maple is ideal for preparing and presenting this salad.

2 cloves garlic
3 tbs. extra virgin olive oil
1 clove garlic, sliced in half, optional
1 tbs. fresh lemon juice
1/8 tsp. freshly ground pepper

1/8 tsp. salt
2 flat anchovy fillets, chopped
1/2 cup *Garlic Croutons*, page 40
1 tbs. freshly grated Parmesan cheese

Carefully wash lettuce, tear into large pieces and set aside. Combine 2 cloves garlic and olive oil in a food processor workbowl or blender container and process until smooth. Rub entire inner surface of a wooden salad bowl with cut garlic, if desired. Pour garlic oil mixture into a small bowl. Add lemon juice, pepper, salt and anchovies. Blend ingredients together. Place lettuce in salad bowl, pour on dressing and *Garlic Croutons*, and toss thoroughly. Sprinkle with freshly grated Parmesan cheese. Serve immediately.

GARLIC CROUTONS

Serve with soups or salads for a spicy treat. This is a clever way to use stale bread.

3 cups (about 6 slices) day-old Italian bread,
   crusts removed, cut into ¾-inch cubes
¼ cup unsalted butter
3 cloves garlic, minced or pressed
½ tsp. dried basil
½ tsp. dried parsley

Prepare bread cubes and set aside. Melt butter in a nonstick skillet over medium heat. Add garlic, basil and parsley. Add bread, reduce heat to medium-low and sauté for 4 to 5 minutes. Stir constantly. Remove from heat and place croutons on baking sheets. Bake in a 325° oven for 25 minutes, or until golden brown. Stir occasionally.

HEARTY LENTIL SALAD

In place of ordinary table salt, use sea salt. It's produced from the evaporation of sea water and contains natural iodine, an essential nutrient. Lentils, an often neglected legume, make this salad hearty and filling.

1/2 cup lentils
1/4 cup olive oil
8 cloves garlic, minced or pressed
1/4 cup chopped red onion
1/2 cup chopped red bell pepper
1/3 cup chopped celery

1/3 cup sliced fresh mushrooms
1/2 cup chopped tomatoes
1 tbs. fresh oregano, or 1 tsp. dried
1 1/2 tsp. fresh mint, or 1/2 tsp. dried
1/4 tsp. freshly ground pepper
1/8 tsp. sea salt

Rinse lentils under cold water. Bring lentils to a boil in water, reduce heat and simmer for 40 minutes. Drain and set aside. Heat olive oil in a large skillet. Add garlic and onion and sauté over low heat for 4 minutes. Add red peppers, celery and mushrooms. Cook over medium-low heat for about 5 minutes, or until vegetables are soft. Add lentils, tomatoes, oregano, mint, pepper and salt. Cover and simmer for 3 minutes, stirring occasionally. Serve hot or cold.

VARIATION
Add 1 cup tomato sauce and serve as a tomato-based side dish or over pasta.

TABOULLEH

This Middle Eastern salad comes together beautifully. The parsley and lemon bring out the wonderful flavors of all the vegetables and spices. Arrange a sampling of taboulleh on a large platter with fresh leafy greens, hummus, marinated olives and grilled pita wedges for an attractive and delicious Mediterranean "antipasto." Serve with fresh pita bread.

$1/2$ cup bulghur wheat
1 cup water
2 cups chopped fresh parsley, firmly packed
1 small cucumber, finely chopped
1 large tomato, finely chopped
3 medium red onions, finely chopped

2 tbs. finely chopped fresh mint
$1/4$ tsp. freshly ground pepper
2 cloves garlic, minced or pressed
$1/4$ cup (about $1 1/2$ lemons) fresh lemon juice
1 tbs. olive or canola oil

Combine bulghur wheat and water and soak for 2 hours. In a large bowl, combine parsley, cucumber, tomato, onions, mint and pepper. Mix thoroughly. Drain bulghur and combine with vegetables and spices. Add garlic and lemon juice. Slowly stir in oil. Mix and refrigerate for at least 3 hours before serving.

TORTELLINI SALAD

This tantalizing vinaigrette melds the flavors of the vegetables and pasta beautifully. For best results, use fresh, crisp, colorful farm stand vegetables.

1 pkg. (14 oz.) fresh or frozen cheese tortellini
1 cup snow peas
4 cups broccoli florets and sliced stems
1 medium red or green bell pepper, cut into $1/2$-inch pieces
3 plum tomatoes, chopped
$1/2$ cup marinated artichokes hearts, drained and quartered
$1/8$ tsp. sea salt
2-4 oz. *Red Raspberry and Garlic Vinaigrette*, page 41

Cook tortellini in a large pot according to package instructions. Rinse under cold water and drain thoroughly. Snip off ends of pea pods. Steam or boil broccoli for 5 minutes and peas for 1 minute; quickly drain and place in ice cold water for 2 to 3 minutes. In a large bowl, combine tortellini, broccoli, peas, pepper, tomatoes, artichoke hearts and salt. Mix thoroughly. Toss with *Red Raspberry and Garlic Vinaigrette.*

PASTA VEGETABLE SALAD

Servings: 6-8

This fresh, light salad is especially delicious on warm summer days — but good anytime.

16 oz. dried tri-colored pasta shells or spirals
1 medium red onion, finely chopped
1 red or green bell pepper, finely chopped
2 large carrots, sliced into $1/8$-inch rounds
2 stalks celery, chopped
$1/8$ tsp. sea salt
2-4 oz. *Garlicky Vinaigrette*, page 42

Cook pasta according to package instructions. Rinse under cold water and drain well. In a large bowl, toss pasta with vegetables, salt and *Garlicky Vinaigrette*. Refrigerate and serve cold.

RED RASPBERRY VINEGAR

Makes about 2½ cups

¼ cup blueberries, fresh or frozen
½ cup red raspberries, fresh or frozen
½ cup cranberries, fresh or frozen
2 cups (16 oz.) white wine vinegar

¼ cup clover honey
2 cinnamon sticks, each 2 inches long
2 whole cloves

Thaw berries if frozen. Bring vinegar to a low boil in a saucepan. Reduce heat to simmer. Add honey, blueberries, ¼ cup raspberries and ¼ cup cranberries. Cool for 1 hour. Strain through a very fine mesh stainless steel strainer or cheesecloth. Pour vinegar into sterilized wine bottles or glass jars. Add remaining berries and spices. Seal containers with tight-fitting corks and store in a dark, dry area for 2 weeks.

RED RASPBERRY AND GARLIC VINAIGRETTE

Makes about ½ cup

Use this special dressing for salads or as a marinade for poultry and seafood.

6 tbs. *Red Raspberry Vinegar*
2 tbs. olive oil
2 cloves garlic, pressed

2 tsp. minced fresh basil
1 tsp. Dijon mustard

Vigorously mix all ingredients in a bowl or bottle. Refrigerate. Shake well to use.

GARLIC VINEGAR

For subtle garlic flavor, substitute this when regular vinegar is called for.

5 cloves garlic, minced or pressed
12 oz. white or red wine vinegar

Combine garlic and vinegar in a clear glass bottle. Carefully seal bottle and store for 2 weeks in a well-lighted area. Strain garlic from vinegar. Store in a cool, dark area.

GARLICKY VINAIGRETTE

Servings: 6

Pour over or toss with a fresh garden salad or cold pasta salad. Also works great as a marinade for meats, poultry, fish or vegetables. Make a fresh batch of vinaigrette each time. Refrigerate; do not store for longer than a day or two.

3 tbs. balsamic vinegar
3/4 cup extra virgin olive oil
1/4 tsp. freshly ground pepper

2 cloves garlic, minced or pressed
2 tsp. chopped fresh basil
1 tbs. fresh lemon juice

In a medium bowl, combine all ingredients and whisk until well blended.

TOMATO GARLIC VINAIGRETTE DRESSING

Servings: 6-8

This is delicious over leafy greens, tomatoes and cucumbers. Mustard lovers can add 1 tbs. Dijon mustard to ingredients for extra flavor.

1 cup tomato juice
2 cloves garlic, minced or pressed
1/4 cup extra virgin olive oil
1/8 tsp. dried basil

1/8 tsp. dried parsley
1/8 tsp. freshly ground pepper
3 tbs. balsamic vinegar

In a medium bowl, combine all ingredients and whisk until well blended. Refrigerate.

BASIC GARLIC
SALAD DRESSING AND MARINADE

Makes 1/3 cup

Serve on antipasto or on a fresh garden salad, or as a marinade for meats.

1/4 cup extra virgin olive oil
2 tbs. white or red wine vinegar
2 cloves garlic, minced or pressed

1/4 tsp. freshly ground pepper
salt to taste

Combine all ingredients in a small bowl and mix together thoroughly.

GARLIC AND HONEY SALAD DRESSING

Servings: 6-8

Enhance the flavor of a well-made salad with this interesting dressing.

2 tbs. white or red wine vinegar
1/4 tsp. sea salt
1/4 tsp. freshly ground pepper
1 clove garlic, minced or pressed

1/2 tsp. Dijon mustard
1 tsp. honey
1/3 cup extra virgin olive oil
1 tbs. chopped fresh basil

Combine vinegar, salt, pepper, garlic, mustard and honey in a small bowl. Mix thoroughly. Slowly add olive oil, stirring constantly. Add basil and blend. Store in an airtight container. Shake before using.

GARLIC-LEMON PEPPERCORNS

Makes about 1/4 cup

Invest in a high-quality pepper mill. Freshly ground pepper will enhance your foods. This flavored pepper adds zest to seafoods, poultry and vegetables.

3 tbs. cracked black peppercorns
2 1/4 tsp. dried minced garlic

1 tsp. dried lemon peel

Mix all ingredients together and grind in a pepper mill or with a mortar and pestle.

VEGETABLES AND SIDE DISHES

ROASTED GARLIC

Roasting garlic mellows its pungency and produces a delicious sweet flavor. I strongly recommend a terra cotta garlic baker with a large diameter so you can roast several bulbs at a time or large elephant garlic bulbs. Serve roasted garlic warm as a spread, or use in other recipes. Increase the recipe size as needed.

1 large bulb garlic
1/4 tsp. or 1 tbs. olive oil (see method)
1 tsp. butter, optional
1/8 tsp. dried basil
1/8 tsp. dried thyme
freshly ground pepper to taste

Heat oven to 350°. For perfectly roasted garlic, cut 1/4 inch from top of garlic bulb. Remove loose outer leaves. Bulb should remain intact. Pour 1/4 tsp. olive oil over bulb and dot with butter, or pour 1 tbs. olive oil over bulb and eliminate butter. Sprinkle with basil, thyme and pepper. Place cover on garlic baker. For a medium to large bulb, bake for 50 minutes. For an extra large bulb, bake for an additional 10 minutes. If cooking in a microwave oven, prepare bulb as directed and cook on HIGH for 1 1/2 minutes. Separate cloves and squeeze out garlic.

AUTHENTIC ROASTED PEPPERS

These are absolutely addictive. Commercially prepared or boiled, skinned roasted peppers just don't compare. Use large thick bell peppers. You can roast the peppers under a broiler or on an outdoor grill. Removing the seeds and stems before roasting makes preparing this dish much easier.

8 large red or green bell peppers
7 cloves garlic, minced or pressed
1 cup olive oil

Leave peppers whole, but cut off tops and remove stems, membranes and all seeds. Rinse under cold water and drain. Place peppers on the grate of a hot grill or under a broiler. With metal tongs, turn peppers every 2 to 3 minutes. Peppers should be charred and blistered in 10 to 12 minutes. Place charred peppers in a brown paper bag. Place filled bag on a platter to prevent wet peppers from breaking through bag. Leave peppers in bag for at least 1 hour, or up to 1 day. Remove peppers and use your fingers to easily peel off blistered skins. Discard skins. Slice peppers into 1½-inch strips and combine with garlic and olive oil. Refrigerate for at least 2 hours. Serve cold.

STUFFED ONIONS WITH ROASTED GARLIC

Servings: 4

An absolutely delightful treat, these are perfect with any main course.

1 bulb garlic, roasted (see page 50)
4 large white onions
3 tbs. butter
2 stalks celery, finely chopped
1 cup seasoned breadcrumbs
1/2 tsp. dried basil

1/4 tsp. dried thyme
1/2 tsp. dried parsley
1/4 tsp. salt
1/4 tsp. freshly ground pepper
3 tbs. grated Parmesan cheese
3 tbs. dry sherry

Squeeze soft garlic into a bowl and mash to form a paste. Set aside. Peel onions and remove ends. Place onions in a large pot of boiling water for 25 minutes. Remove and cool for 15 minutes. Cut onions in half horizontally and remove centers, leaving a shell of 3 to 4 layers of onion. If shells are thin, add back some center pieces to thicken. Mince remaining onion centers (about 1/4 cup) and set aside.

Heat oven to 400°. Prepare stuffing: Melt butter in a skillet. Add celery and sauté for 5 to 7 minutes, or until tender. Add minced onion centers and garlic paste and sauté for 4 minutes. Add breadcrumbs, basil, thyme, parsley, salt, pepper, Parmesan cheese and sherry. Mix thoroughly and sauté on medium heat for 4 minutes. Place hollowed onions in an ovenproof casserole. Fill centers with stuffing. Bake uncovered for 30 minutes.

ROASTED GARLIC AND SPINACH QUICHE

Servings: 6

Serve this crustless quiche as a side dish or for luncheon as the main attraction. To assure a perfect texture, carefully drain cooked spinach of all water.

1 bulb garlic, roasted (see page 50)
1 tbs. butter
1 small onion, finely chopped
4 eggs
1 cup milk
1/4 tsp. chili powder

1/2 tsp. salt
1/4 tsp. freshly ground pepper
1 cup cooked spinach, fresh or frozen, drained well
1/2 cup shredded Monterey Jack cheese
1/4 tsp. vegetable oil for oiling pan

Heat oven to 350°. Separate roasted garlic cloves, peel and mash in a small bowl to form a paste. Melt butter in a skillet. Add onion and sauté until soft, about 6 minutes. Add garlic paste and sauté for 4 minutes. Blend together and set aside. In a medium bowl, whisk together eggs, milk, chili powder, salt and pepper. In another bowl, combine garlic-onion mixture with spinach and cheese. Mix well. Spread spinach mixture firmly in a lightly oiled 9-inch quiche or pie pan. Pour egg mixture evenly over spinach.

Bake for 40 minutes. Quiche is done when a toothpick inserted in the center comes out clean.

MARINARA SAUCE

This appetizing sauce is delicious with pasta and other cooked foods.

2 tbs. olive oil
3 cloves garlic, minced or pressed
1 medium onion, finely chopped
2 cans (28 oz. each) Italian plum tomatoes, chopped and mashed
$1/2$ tsp. dried oregano
2 tbs. chopped fresh basil
$1/4$ tsp. freshly ground pepper
$1/8$ tsp. salt

Heat olive oil in a medium saucepan over medium heat. Add garlic and onion and sauté for 5 to 7 minutes, or until onions are soft. Add tomatoes. Stir in oregano, basil, pepper and salt. Partially cover saucepan. Reduce heat and simmer for $1 1/2$ hours. Stir occasionally.

ROASTED GARLIC BREAD

Servings: 8

This specially flavored bread is well worth the effort. Roasted garlic and a stick of freshly baked bread are just meant to be eaten together.

2 bulbs garlic, roasted (see page 50)
1 tbs. olive oil
2 tbs. freshly grated Parmesan cheese
½ tsp. dried basil

¼ tsp. dried oregano
¼ tsp. dried parsley
¼ tsp. freshly ground pepper
1 loaf Italian bread or French baguette

Heat oven to 350°. Separate roasted garlic cloves, peel and mash in a small bowl to form a paste. Combine garlic paste with all remaining ingredients, except bread. Mix thoroughly. Slice bread in half lengthwise, separating top from bottom. Spread garlic mixture on inside of each half. Wrap each half in parchment paper or foil and bake for 10 minutes. Remove parchment paper or foil wrap from bread and place under the broiler for 2 to 3 minutes.

VARIATION

Slice bread at an angle, ¾ through, at 1-inch intervals. Spread garlic mixture between bread slices. Wrap bread with foil and bake in a 350° oven for 20 minutes. Serve warm.

FRESH VEGETABLE AND GARLIC MEDLEY

This dish proves you can have delicious food that is also good for you!

4 cloves garlic, thinly sliced
3 large carrots, peeled, cut into matchstick strips
1 medium zucchini, cut into matchstick strips
1 medium tomato, diced
1 medium red bell pepper, cut into matchstick strips
1 tbs. chopped fresh basil
1/2 tsp. freshly ground pepper
2 tbs. low-sodium soy sauce

Combine all ingredients in a large bowl. Marinate in the refrigerator for 2 hours.

Heat oven to 375°. Lay out two 18-x-15-inch sheets of parchment paper and fold in half. Open sheets of parchment paper and place half the ingredients on one side of each sheet, next to the fold. Fold and tightly seal packets by overlapping small 1/4-inch folds or a series of long, thin folds along the sides. Place packets on a baking sheet and bake for 20 minutes. Transfer cooked vegetables to a large serving bowl or individual plates.

GRILLED ZUCCHINI

Servings: 4

Garlicky Vinaigrette *is used as a marinade with fresh zucchini. Serve as a side dish or as a main course with a marinara sauce and pasta.*

8 tender young zucchini
16 oz. *Garlicky Vinaigrette*, page 46

Slice zucchini in half lengthwise into 2 thick pieces. Place zucchini in a shallow bowl and cover with marinade. Cover and refrigerate for 4 hours, turning occasionally in marinade. Cook on a barbecue grill rack over medium-high heat for 10 to 12 minutes on each side, basting frequently with marinade, or cook under a broiler for 6 to 7 minutes on each side.

FRESH SPINACH WITH GARLIC

Servings: 4-6

Spinach is great with garlic. But spinach does not store very well. Buy it fresh and cook it within two days. This is a perfect accompaniment for a seafood dish.

3/4 lb. fresh spinach
1/3 cup olive oil
4 cloves garlic, thinly sliced
1/2 tsp. dried basil
1/2 tsp. freshly ground pepper

Wash spinach thoroughly under cold running water. Be sure to remove all the grit. Cut out tough stems and leave spinach whole or break into large pieces. Place spinach in a medium saucepan in 1 inch water. Pour olive oil over spinach. Mix in garlic slices and sprinkle with basil and pepper. Bring to a boil. Cover, reduce heat to medium and cook for 5 to 7 minutes, or until tender. Serve in individual serving bowls with garlic-flavored liquid.

HARVEST SUN MIXED VEGETABLES

Servings: 4

The secret to this recipe is the fennel. It adds a distinctive licorice flavor to the dish. Fennel looks like celery and in some regions it is mislabeled as sweet anise.

2 tbs. canola or olive oil
4 cloves garlic, minced or pressed
1 medium onion, thinly sliced
1 bulb fennel, thinly sliced
1 medium zucchini, cut into
  $1/4$-inch rounds
1 medium red bell pepper, cut into
  1-inch pieces

2 cups broccoli florets and sliced
  stems
$1/4$ cup water
$1/2$ tsp. dried thyme
1 tsp. freshly ground pepper
juice of $1/2$ lemon

Heat oil in a deep skillet over low-medium heat. Add garlic and onion and sauté for 4 minutes. Add fennel, cover and cook for 5 minutes. Add zucchini, red pepper, broccoli, water, thyme and pepper. Cover and cook over medium heat for 10 to 12 minutes. Place cooked vegetables in a large serving bowl or on individual serving plates. Drizzle with lemon juice and serve immediately.

ARTICHOKES WITH GARLIC STUFFING

Servings: 4

Serve hot or cold as an appetizer or side dish.

4 medium artichokes
8 slices day-old Italian or country-style bread, 1 inch thick, crust removed
2 cloves garlic, minced or pressed
1/4 tsp. dried basil
1/2 cup olive oil
1/4 tsp. freshly ground pepper
2 tbs. grated Parmesan cheese

Remove 1 inch from artichoke stems and 1/2 inch from tops. Remove tough bottom leaves and snip off points on all leaves. Open space between leaves by banging artichoke tops on the counter, or stretch open area between layers of leaves. Rinse artichokes under cold running water and drain upside down.

Prepare stuffing: Cut bread into 1-inch cubes. In a large bowl, thoroughly mix together bread, garlic, basil, olive oil, pepper and Parmesan cheese. Starting with the second row of outer leaves, put a small amount of stuffing inside each leaf.

Place artichokes in an upright position in a large pot with 1 inch water. Bring water to a boil, cover and reduce heat to low. Cook for 35 to 45 minutes. When leaves are removed easily, artichokes are done.

SAUTÉED BRUSSELS SPROUTS WITH GARLIC

Servings: 4

Bright green Brussels sprouts complement the mushrooms and pepper beautifully for an eye-appealing and tasty dish.

1 lb. fresh Brussels sprouts
2 tbs. vegetable or canola oil
3 cloves garlic, minced or pressed
1 cup thinly sliced mushrooms
1 red bell pepper, cut into matchstick strips
2 tbs. *Garlic Herb Butter*, page 23
1/4 cup roasted pecans or cashews, optional

Remove outer leaves and cut Brussels sprouts into quarters. Heat oil in a large skillet. Add garlic and sauté for 1 minute. Add Brussels sprouts, mushrooms and pepper. Sauté for 5 to 7 minutes. Transfer to a serving bowl and toss with *Garlic Herb Butter*. For added flavor and crunch, sprinkle with roasted pecans or cashews after cooking.

STRING BEAN AND GARLIC MIX

This deeply flavorful vegetable dish tastes great hot or cold. It's a good addition to a picnic, and it's easy to prepare, too.

1 lb. string beans
3 tbs. olive oil
3/4 tsp. garlic powder
1/4 tsp. dried basil
freshly ground pepper to taste

Snip tips off both ends of beans with kitchen shears or cut off with a sharp knife. Break beans in half and wash under cold running water. Place beans in a 2½- to 3½-quart saucepan with 1 inch water and steam or boil until tender, about 4 minutes. Remove beans, without liquid, from saucepan. If you are serving them cold, plunge beans into cold water for 1 to 2 minutes, drain and place in a storage container or bowl. If you are serving them hot, remove to a serving bowl. Add olive oil, garlic powder, basil and pepper. Mix thoroughly. Serve hot or refrigerate and serve cold.

GARLICKY VEGETABLE SAUTÉ

This spicy and satisfying vegetable recipe can easily be increased if you need more servings.

2 tbs. olive or vegetable oil
$1/2$ tsp. paprika
$1/2$ cup sliced scallions
4 cloves garlic, minced or pressed
1 medium red bell pepper, cut into thin matchstick strips
1 medium green bell pepper, cut into thin matchstick strips
1 medium yellow summer squash, sliced into $1/8$-inch rounds
1 medium zucchini, sliced into $1/8$-inch rounds
$1/4$ tsp. freshly ground pepper

Heat oil in a large skillet over medium heat. Add paprika and stir thoroughly. Add scallions and garlic; sauté for 2 minutes. Add all other ingredients, partially cover and sauté over medium-low heat for 15 to 17 minutes, or until vegetables are tender, stirring occasionally.

BROCCOLI AND GARLIC STIR-FRY

Serve as a side dish with meats, poultry or seafood. It's also exceptionally flavorful as an entrée over white rice on individual serving plates.

1 lb. fresh broccoli florets and stems
2 tsp. sesame seeds
1 tbs. safflower, sunflower or peanut oil
6 cloves garlic, minced or pressed
$1/2$ tsp. grated fresh ginger
1 tbs. low-sodium soy sauce
$1/4$ cup water

Chop broccoli florets into 1-inch pieces and cut stems into matchstick strips. Roast sesame seeds in a dry skillet over medium heat, stirring constantly, until seeds are golden brown. Heat oil over medium-high heat in a skillet or wok. Add garlic and fresh ginger and sauté for 1 minute. Add broccoli, soy sauce and water. Stir-fry for 4 minutes. Transfer broccoli to a serving bowl and mix in sesame seeds.

GARLIC AND HONEY CARROTS

Choose young, tender carrots for a sweet, full flavor. You'll cook this dish again!

3 cups carrots, cut into ¼-inch rounds
2 tbs. butter
1 tbs. honey
1 clove garlic, minced or pressed
1 tsp. minced onion
2 tbs. raisins
1 tsp. brown sugar, packed
¼ tsp. dried dill weed

Place carrots in a vegetable steamer with 1 inch water. Bring to a boil and steam for 5 to 7 minutes, or until carrots are tender-crisp.

Make sauce: While carrots are cooking, combine, butter, honey, garlic, onion, raisins, brown sugar and dill weed in a small saucepan. Cook over low heat until onion and garlic are soft.

Combine carrots and sauce in a serving bowl. Mix thoroughly. Serve warm.

ITALIAN VEGETABLE STIR-FRY

This recipe combines an authentic Italian flavor with a quick and easy Asian technique. Serve it as an entrée over polenta, rice or noodles, or as a side dish.

2 tbs. canola oil
1 red onion, cut into 16 wedges
1 yellow pepper, cut into matchstick
    strips
1 bunch broccoli, cut into 1-inch pieces
6 cloves garlic, crushed or pressed
1/4 cup water
2 tbs. tomato paste
1 can (14 oz.) diced tomatoes, with
    juice

1/3 cup chopped sun-dried tomatoes,
    reconstituted
2/3 cup roasted red peppers, cut into
    matchstick strips (see page 51)
1/4 cup chopped fresh basil
1 tsp. dried oregano, or 1 tbs. chopped
    fresh
1 tbs. balsamic vinegar
salt and pepper to taste
1/4 cup grated Parmesan cheese

Heat wok or stir-fry pan over medium-high heat. Add canola oil and heat for 30 seconds. Add onions, yellow peppers and broccoli and stir-fry for 5 to 6 minutes. Add garlic and stir-fry for 30 seconds. Add water and tomato paste and mix well. Add diced tomatoes and heat thoroughly. Add sun-dried tomatoes, roasted red peppers, basil and oregano and mix well. Cook until heated through, about 2 to 3 minutes. Add balsamic vinegar, salt and pepper. Mix well. Serve sprinkled with Parmesan.

HEAVENLY RICE AND SPINACH

Leave standard potatoes or plain cooked rice behind! This adventurous side dish has an extraordinary rich flavor.

1/8 cup toasted pine nuts, optional
1 1/2 cups long-grain white rice
5 tbs. butter
6 cloves garlic, minced or pressed
2 medium onions, finely chopped

1/4 tsp. salt
1/4 tsp. freshly ground pepper
4 cups chopped fresh spinach, packed
3/4 cup chicken stock
1/2 cup freshly grated Parmesan cheese

Roast pine nuts in a dry skillet over medium heat, stirring constantly until golden brown. Set aside. Prepare rice according to package instructions. Melt butter in a large skillet. Add garlic and onions and sauté for 5 minutes. Add salt, pepper and spinach and sauté for 3 minutes, or until spinach becomes limp. Add chicken stock and cooked rice. Sauté for 5 minutes, or until rice is steaming hot. Stir in Parmesan cheese and toasted pine nuts. Remove from heat. Keep covered and serve warm.

STUFFED BAKED POTATOES

Servings: 4

The roasted garlic stuffing blends very nicely with the Parmesan cheese for a perfectly flavored potato.

8 cloves garlic, roasted (see page 50)
4 large baking potatoes
2 tsp. minced fresh or freeze-dried chives
1/2 cup milk
1/4 cup butter, melted
3 tbs. grated Parmesan cheese

Heat oven to 450°. Squeeze soft garlic into a small bowl and mash. Set aside. Carefully scrub potatoes under cold running water with a vegetable brush to remove dirt. Place potatoes in the oven for 50 minutes. Slice potatoes in half lengthwise and carefully scoop out pulp without breaking skins. Mash or press pulp through a vegetable ricer. In a medium bowl, combine pulp with garlic, chives, milk, melted butter and 1 tbs. of the Parmesan cheese. Mix well. Refill potato skins with stuffing.

Reduce oven temperature to 400°. Place potatoes in an ovenproof dish and sprinkle tops with remaining 2 tbs. Parmesan cheese. Bake for 10 minutes. Place under a hot broiler for 4 minutes, or until golden brown. Serve immediately.

GARLIC-ROASTED POTATOES

Servings: 4

You can prepare these irresistible potatoes for any occasion. I recommend using a medium-sized freezer bag for coating the potatoes with the seasonings.

1 ½ lb. new red-skinned potatoes
¼ cup olive oil
4 large cloves garlic, minced or pressed
½ tsp. dried basil
½ tsp. dried oregano
¼ tsp. freshly ground pepper

Heat oven to 425°. Wash potatoes under cold running water with a vegetable brush. Remove eyes, but do not peel. Cut into 1-inch cubes. In a medium-sized plastic bag, combine all ingredients. Shake until potatoes are evenly coated. Place potatoes in a single layer in an ovenproof baking dish. Bake for 50 minutes. Turn occasionally.

POTATO FANTASY

Servings: 4

This new-style potato side dish goes especially well with lamb or beef.

2 tbs. flour
8 medium new potatoes
2 tbs. butter
2 tbs. olive oil
4 cloves garlic, minced or pressed
½ cup chopped scallions
2 stalks celery, finely chopped

1 cup thinly sliced mushrooms
¾ cup chicken broth
3 tbs. chopped fresh basil
2 tsp. honey
1½ tsp. Italian herbs
⅛ tsp. salt
fresh parsley for garnish

Brown flour in a dry skillet over medium heat, stirring occasionally, for 8 minutes and set aside. Boil potatoes for 18 minutes, or until tender. Drain and submerge potatoes in cold water. Slice or dice potatoes and set aside.

Heat butter and olive oil in a deep skillet. Sauté garlic for 2 minutes over medium heat. Add scallions, celery and mushrooms. Sauté for 3 minutes. Add chicken broth, basil, honey, Italian herbs and salt. As soon as liquid begins to boil, slowly whisk in flour. Add potatoes and simmer for 3 to 5 minutes, or until potatoes are warm. Mix thoroughly and serve at room temperature with sprigs of fresh parsley.

MASHED POTATOES WITH ROASTED GARLIC
Servings: 6-8

I prefer to mash the potatoes with an old-fashioned hand masher because I like my potatoes slightly lumpy. If you're not a fan of lumpy potatoes, process the ingredients with an electric mixer until lump-free and fluffy.

1 medium bulb garlic, roasted (see
    page 50)
2 lb. potatoes, about 6
$\frac{1}{2}$ cup milk

$\frac{1}{4}$ cup butter
$\frac{1}{4}$ tsp. freshly ground pepper
chopped fresh parsley, optional

Prepare roasted garlic. Peel potatoes and cut into quarters. Place potatoes in a deep pot of cold water. Water should just cover potatoes. Cover pot and bring to a boil. Reduce heat and simmer for 20 minutes, or until tender. Carefully drain potatoes. Heat potatoes in pot over low heat to dry, stirring or shaking continuously.

Mash potatoes with a strong masher. Slowly add milk and mash continuously. Squeeze roasted garlic from each clove and add to potatoes with butter and pepper. Mash thoroughly. Transfer to serving plates or a warm ceramic bowl. Garnish with chopped parsley. For best flavor, serve immediately.

PASTA

SPAGHETTI WITH GARLIC AND BASIL CREAM SAUCE

The Ancient Greeks referred to basil as the "royal herb." This delicious sauce transforms the pasta into a gourmet's delight.

6 oz. dried spaghetti
1/4 cup butter
4 cloves garlic, minced or pressed
1 cup light cream
1 tbs. plus 1 tsp. minced fresh basil
1/8 tsp. dried thyme
1/8 tsp. freshly ground pepper
freshly grated Parmesan cheese

Cook spaghetti in a medium pot according to package instructions. Melt butter in a small deep skillet. Add garlic and sauté for 3 minutes over low heat. Pour in cream and add 1 tbs. basil, thyme and pepper. Stir thoroughly. Simmer over medium-low heat, covered but vented, for 7 to 9 minutes, or until thickened. Stir occasionally. If sauce becomes too thick, add more cream to thin. Pour sauce over spaghetti and sprinkle with fresh basil. Serve immediately with Parmesan cheese.

ROASTED VEGETABLES OVER LINGUINE

Servings: 4

Roasting allows the vegetables to maintain their distinctive flavors. This beautiful dish goes great with a fresh garden salad and lots of fresh Italian bread.

1 bulb garlic, roasted (see page 50)
1 medium eggplant
1 large red bell pepper
1 large green bell pepper
1 large red onion
2 medium zucchini
2 medium yellow crookneck squash
1/4 cup olive oil
1/4 cup balsamic vinegar
1 cup water
1 chicken bouillon cube
16 oz. dried linguine
2 tbs. chopped fresh basil
1/2 cup freshly grated Parmesan cheese

Heat oven to 425°. Prepare roasted garlic. Peel eggplant and cut into ½-inch cubes. Remove stems, membranes and all seeds from peppers and cut lengthwise into ¼-inch-wide slices. Cut onion into quarters and separate layers. Slice zucchini and yellow crookneck squash into ¼-inch rounds. Pierce roasted garlic with a fork to easily remove cooked cloves from skin. In a large bowl, combine garlic, eggplant, pepper, onion, zucchini and squash with olive oil and vinegar. Mix thoroughly.

Arrange vegetables in a metal roasting or baking pan. Bake for 30 minutes. Stir occasionally. Place vegetables under a hot broiler for 3 minutes. Heat 1 cup water over low heat and dissolve bouillon cube. Cook linguine in a large pot according to package instructions. Drain pasta and return to pot. Add chicken bouillon, stir and keep warm over low heat. Arrange linguine on 4 warm serving plates. Divide roasted vegetables over pasta. Sprinkle with fresh basil and Parmesan cheese and serve immediately.

BOW TIE PASTA WITH
ROASTED GARLIC AND EGGPLANT

The fontina cheese melts from the heat of the cooked vegetables and pasta for a truly wonderful dish with an interesting roasted flavor.

1 bulb garlic, roasted (see page 50)
6 cups eggplant, peeled and cut into 1-inch cubes
1/2 cup balsamic vinegar
4 tbs. olive oil
1/4 tsp. dried oregano
1/2 tsp. freshly ground pepper
3 cups chopped tomatoes , about 3 medium tomatoes
1 pkg. (8 oz.) dried large bow tie pasta
1/2 cup shredded fontina cheese
2 tbs. chopped fresh parsley
1/4 cup freshly grated Parmesan cheese

Heat oven to 425°. Separate roasted garlic cloves, peel and set aside. In a medium bowl, combine eggplant, vinegar, 3 tbs. olive oil, oregano and pepper. Mix thoroughly and marinate in the refrigerator for 1 hour. Place eggplant with liquid in a baking pan and bake for 25 minutes. Stir every 5 to 6 minutes.

About 10 minutes before eggplant is completely cooked, heat 1 tbs. olive oil in a skillet. Add tomatoes and garlic. Sauté for 5 minutes.

At the same time, cook pasta according to package instructions. Drain and divide cooked pasta on 4 serving plates. Cover pasta with roasted eggplant. Sprinkle with fontina cheese. Cover cheese with equal portions of tomato-garlic mixture and top with parsley. Serve immediately sprinkled with Parmesan cheese.

PAD THAI

Pad Thai is the most famous Thai noodle dish. Unlike Chinese cooking, where the ingredients are in constant motion, in Thai cooking the initial ingredients are stir-fried, but once all of the ingredients and liquid have been added, the tossing is reduced to a gentle stir to prevent ruining the texture of the delicate noodles and vegetables.

½ lb. dried rice flour noodles, about
   ¼-inch thick
3 tbs. canola oil
3 cloves garlic, minced or pressed
7 cups water
1 tbs. brown sugar
2 tbs. soy sauce
2 tbs. fish sauce
2 eggs, lightly beaten

s4 medium shrimp, peeled and
   deveined
1 lb. skinless, boneless chicken, cut
   into 3-inch strips
2 tsp. paprika
2 cups bean sprouts
1 tbs. skinless roasted unsalted
   peanuts, crushed
4 scallions, cut into 1-inch pieces
½ lime, cut into wedges

Place 6 cups of the water in a wok or stir-fry pan and bring to a boil. Add noodles; cook 3 to 4 minutes or until tender, but still firm; stir frequently. Be careful not to overcook noodles. Drain in a colander and rinse under cold running water to stop cooking. Place drained noodles in a large bowl and coat with 1/2 tbs. of the oil. Set aside.

Combine remaining 1 cup water, brown sugar, soy sauce and fish sauce in a small bowl and set aside. Heat pan over medium heat until hot, about 30 seconds. Add 1/2 tbs. of the oil and heat. Add egg and cook until set, about 1 minute. Stir to scramble. Transfer to a medium bowl and set aside.

Heat pan over high heat until hot. Add 1/2 tbs. of the oil to pan. Add shrimp, chicken and garlic; stir-fry for about 2 to 3 minutes or until cooked. Transfer shrimp and chicken to bowl with egg. Heat pan over medium heat until hot. Add remaining tablespoon of oil to pan and heat. Stir in paprika. Increase heat to medium-high; add sprouts and scallions and stir-fry for 1 to 2 minutes or until scallions start to wilt. Add egg, shrimp and chicken and stir-fry until heated through. Add cooked noodles and fish sauce mixture; gently mix well. Transfer to a large platter and top with crushed peanuts. Garnish with lime wedges.

PASTA WITH BASIL, GARLIC AND TOMATOES

If you're cooking with canned chicken broth, use a gravy separator to eliminate the excess fat. You can also pour the broth into a bowl or other container and refrigerate it until the fat solidifies, and then lift the fat from the broth. For added flavor, substitute dried basil with 3 tbs. chopped fresh basil.

12 oz. dried angel hair pasta
2 tbs. olive oil
8 cloves garlic, thinly sliced
2 cups chicken broth

4 cups chopped plum tomatoes
1 tbs. dried basil
freshly grated Parmesan or Romano
  cheese

Cook angel hair pasta in a large pot of boiling water for 2 to 3 minutes. Do not overcook. Drain well and set aside. Heat olive oil in a deep 3- to 4-quart skillet over medium heat. Add garlic slices and reduce heat to low. Sauté garlic until tender, about 3 to 5 minutes, but do not brown. Add chicken broth and tomato pieces, increase heat and bring to a boil. Reduce heat to low. Cover skillet and simmer for 7 minutes. Stir in basil and cook for 1 more minute. Distribute cooked pasta on 4 warm serving plates. Carefully spoon tomato-garlic mixture over pasta. Coat all pasta with seasoned liquid. Sprinkle with Parmesan or Romano cheese.

PASTA WITH TOMATO AND GARLIC SAUCE

The garlic provides a stimulating flavor to this classic pasta entrée.

2 tbs. olive oil
12 cloves garlic, minced or pressed
1 cup minced onion
1 can (28 oz.) tomato puree
3 tbs. minced fresh basil
1 tsp. minced fresh parsley

$\frac{1}{4}$ freshly ground pepper
$\frac{1}{8}$ tsp. sugar
1 large bay leaf
12 oz. dried fettuccine or linguine
freshly grated Parmesan or Romano
   cheese

Heat olive oil in a saucepan or deep skillet. Add garlic and onion; sauté over medium heat for 7 to 10 minutes, or until soft. Add tomato puree and stir in remaining ingredients, except cheese. Simmer with lid vented over medium-low heat for 1$\frac{1}{2}$ hours. Stir occasionally. Cook pasta according to package instructions. Remove bay leaf from sauce. Pour sauce over pasta and serve sprinkled with cheese.

PASTA WITH BROCCOLI

This is one of my personal favorites — quick, easy and very tasty. Pasta is always good with fresh Italian bread and a large garden salad.

1 lb. dried macaroni
6 cloves garlic, minced or pressed
1/2 cup olive oil
4 cups broccoli florets and sliced stems
1/2 cup freshly grated Parmesan cheese

Cook macaroni in a large 5- to 6-quart pot of boiling water according to package instructions. Do not overcook. Drain well.

While macaroni is cooking, combine garlic and olive oil in a small saucepan and sauté over low heat for 8 minutes. Steam broccoli in a 2- to 3-quart covered saucepan for 5 minutes. Combine cooked pasta, steamed broccoli and garlic oil mixture in pot. Mix well and cook over low heat for 5 more minutes. Stir occasionally. Serve hot with Parmesan cheese.

PASTA AND GARLIC CHEESE SAUCE

Servings: 4

For variety, substitute another vegetable for broccoli, or eliminate it and increase the quantity of pasta. Serve as a main course or side dish.

4 cups broccoli florets and sliced stems
16 oz. dried rigatoni, or small shells
1 tbs. olive oil
2 tbs. butter
3 tbs. flour
1 cup milk
1 tbs. fresh garlic, minced or pressed
1 tbs. minced onion

2 tsp. dried basil
1 tsp. dried thyme
1/2 tsp. freshly ground pepper
1 cup shredded fontina cheese
1 cup shredded mozzarella cheese
freshly grated Parmesan cheese,
  optional

Cook broccoli in a vegetable steamer, or boil for 5 to 6 minutes, and set aside.

Cook pasta in a large pot according to package instructions. Drain pasta and return to pot. Toss pasta with olive oil and cooked broccoli. In a medium saucepan, melt butter over medium heat. Stir continuously, slowly adding flour and milk. Add garlic, onion, basil, thyme and pepper. Mix well. Add fontina and mozzarella cheeses, mixing continuously over low heat as sauce forms, about 1 to 2 minutes. Pour sauce over pasta and broccoli. Serve immediately topped with Parmesan cheese.

PASTA WITH ROASTED GARLIC AND GREEN PEPPERS

Servings: 4

For a colorful appearance, prepare this dish with spinach fettuccine. You can replace the sauce with your own recipe or a favorite commercially prepared brand. Serve with fresh Italian or French bread.

2 bulbs garlic, roasted (see page 50)
2 tbs. olive oil
1 large green or red bell pepper, diced
1 onion, minced
1 tsp. dried basil
$\frac{1}{2}$ tsp. dried oregano
$\frac{1}{4}$ tsp. freshly ground pepper
4 cups *Marinara Sauce*, page 54
12 oz. dried fettuccine
freshly grated Parmesan cheese

Squeeze soft garlic from each roasted garlic clove and set aside. Heat olive oil in a skillet and sauté bell pepper for 3 minutes. Add onion and continue to sauté for 5 more minutes. Add pepper, onion, garlic and spices to *Marinara Sauce* and simmer for 30 minutes. Stir occasionally.

Cook pasta in a large pot of boiling water according to package instructions. Drain well. Distribute cooked pasta on warm serving plates. Top with a layer of sauce. Pass Parmesan cheese.

FETTUCCINE WITH GARLIC OIL

Serve as a main course or side dish with veal, poultry or seafood. For the best flavor, purchase Parmesan or Romano cheese in a large piece and grate it easily at home with a food processor or with a stainless steel hand crank-style grater.

2/3 cup olive oil
10 cloves garlic
12 oz. dried fettuccine
1/3 cup chopped fresh parsley
freshly grated Parmesan or Romano cheese

In a small saucepan, heat olive oil over medium heat. Add whole garlic cloves, reduce heat to low, cover and simmer for 25 minutes. Strain garlic and save oil. Set garlic aside to cool.

Cook pasta in a large pot according to package instructions. While pasta is cooking, squeeze pulp from garlic cloves and mash. Drain pasta and return to pot. Toss pasta with oil, garlic and parsley. Top with Parmesan or Romano cheese.

PASTA WITH ROASTED GARLIC
AND BASIL SAUCE

Serve as a main course or side dish with a salad and garlic bread. The highly aromatic sauce is also delicious over freshly cooked vegetables.

10 cloves garlic
1/4 cup plus 1/4 tsp. safflower, sunflower
   or vegetable oil
1 tbs. balsamic vinegar
1 cup chopped fresh basil
1/4 cup chopped fresh parsley

1/4 cup chopped walnuts, or pine nuts
3 tbs. chicken broth
1/2 tsp. freshly ground pepper
2 tbs. freshly grated Parmesan cheese
12 oz. dried linguine

Heat oven to 350°. Place garlic cloves in a garlic baker or on a nonstick or lightly oiled baking sheet. Cover and bake for 30 to 35 minutes. Peel skin from garlic cloves, or squeeze out garlic pulp.

Combine garlic, 1/4 cup of the oil, vinegar, basil, parsley, nuts, chicken broth and pepper in a food processor workbowl or blender container and process until smooth. Transfer to a bowl and stir in cheese; set aside or refrigerate. Cook pasta according to package instructions. Rinse pasta and drain. Remove pasta to a saucepan over low heat. Toss with garlic-basil mixture and serve.

FISH AND SHELLFISH

BAKED STUFFED SHRIMP

Roasted garlic and shrimp combine perfectly for a spectacular meal.

1 bulb garlic, roasted (see page 50)
3 tbs. butter
1/4 cup finely chopped green bell
    pepper
1 small onion, finely chopped
1/2 cup breadcrumbs

1/4 tsp. dried thyme
1/4 tsp. freshly ground pepper
1/4 tsp. salt
2 tbs. freshly grated Parmesan cheese
8 jumbo shrimp, peeled and deveined
3 tbs. butter, melted

Heat oven to 400°. Separate roasted garlic cloves, peel and mash in a small bowl to form a paste. Melt butter in a skillet over medium heat. Add green pepper and onion and sauté for 4 minutes. Add garlic paste and sauté for 3 minutes. Add breadcrumbs, thyme, pepper and salt and sauté for 3 minutes. Add Parmesan cheese. Mix well and allow to cool.

Butterfly shrimp and place in an ovenproof baking dish. Roll stuffing into eight 1 1/4-inch balls. Place a ball of stuffing on top of each shrimp. Drizzle with melted butter. Bake for 7 to 10 minutes, or until shrimp are pink. Serve immediately.

SAUTÉED SHRIMP WITH GARLIC AND ONION

Servings: 4

A shrimp cleaner is inexpensive and easy to use, and will greatly reduce the time spent preparing this and other shrimp recipes. Serve this dish with pasta and salad.

2 lb. fresh or frozen large shrimp
1 tsp. paprika
½ tsp. dried thyme
½ tsp. dried chervil
¼ tsp. dried marjoram
¼ tsp. ground sea salt
1 tsp. freshly ground pepper

1 tsp. plus 2 tbs. butter
6 cloves garlic, minced or pressed
1 medium onion, minced
1 tbs. fresh lemon juice
1 lemon, cut into wedges
1 tbs. minced fresh basil

Peel and devein shrimp. Wash under cold running water, drain and dry with paper towels. In a small bowl, combine paprika, thyme, chervil, marjoram, salt and pepper. Toss shrimp with herbs and set aside.

Heat 1 tsp. butter in a large skillet over medium heat and sauté garlic and onion until lightly browned, about 3 minutes. Remove from skillet and set aside.

Heat 2 tbs. butter in skillet and sauté shrimp for 2 minutes. Add garlic, onion and lemon juice and sauté for 1 minute. Transfer to individual serving plates, each with a few lemon wedges. Sprinkle with fresh basil and serve.

SHRIMP AND GARLIC STIR-FRY

Servings: 4

This makes a gratifying meal full of flavor and lavish colors. Most of the preparation can be done in advance, so the cook can relax and enjoy the evening. Serve over pasta or fresh lettuce for a variation.

1/4 cup almond slices
2 tbs. peanut or vegetable oil
2 tbs. butter
2 stalks celery, cut diagonally into
  1/4-inch slices
1/2 cup sliced scallions
6 cloves garlic, minced or pressed
2 cloves garlic, thinly sliced

1 red bell pepper, cut into matchstick
  strips
1 medium zucchini, cut into matchstick
  strips
1/2 cup dried sun-dried tomato pieces
1 lb. large shrimp, peeled and
  deveined
steamed white rice

Toast almond slices in a dry skillet over medium heat, stirring constantly until golden brown; set aside. Heat oil and butter in a large skillet or wok over medium heat. Add celery, scallions and all of the garlic. Sauté for 3 minutes. Add pepper, zucchini and sun-dried tomatoes and mix. Cover and simmer over low heat for 5 minutes. Add shrimp. Stir and sauté over medium-high heat until shrimp turn pink, about 2 to 3 minutes. Serve over rice. Scatter almond slices on top.

SHRIMP SCAMPI

Absolutely delightful! This dish has 70 percent less fat than most scampi recipes and is just as flavorful.

1 medium bulb garlic, roasted for 45 minutes (see page 50)
1 lb. fresh or frozen large shrimp
2 tbs. butter
4 cloves garlic, minced or pressed
2 tbs. olive oil
1/3 cup dry sherry

2 tbs. fresh lemon juice
1 tbs. chopped fresh parsley
1/4 tsp. salt, optional
6 oz. spinach fettuccine, cooked according to package instructions, optional

Heat oven to 450°. Squeeze roasted garlic into a small bowl and set aside. Peel and devein shrimp. Wash under cold running water and pat dry. Melt butter in a small saucepan. Add minced garlic, olive oil, sherry, lemon juice, parsley and salt. Place shrimp in a shallow ovenproof baking dish. Do not allow shrimp to overlap. Arrange roasted garlic cloves among shrimp. Pour sauce over shrimp and garlic cloves. Bake for 5 minutes. Place under a preheated broiler for 5 minutes. Serve immediately on warm individual serving plates or over hot spinach fettuccine.

BAKED LEMON SOLE
WITH SEAFOOD STUFFING

This quick and easy low-fat sauce is a tasty addition to any baked or grilled fish.

4 sole fillets, 6 oz. each
1 tbs. butter
1/2 cup finely chopped celery
1/3 cup finely chopped onion
3 cloves garlic, pressed or minced
1 1/4 cups dry bread cubes
3 tbs. hot water

1 tsp. fresh grated lemon zest
1/4 lb. cooked shrimp, chopped
1/4 lb. cooked lobster, chopped
salt and pepper to taste
chopped fresh chives for garnish
fresh whole chives for garnish
lemon slices for garnish

Heat oven to 375°. Melt butter in a large skillet over medium heat. Sauté onion and celery until onion is soft. Add garlic and sauté for 1 minute. Remove from heat. In a medium bowl, toss bread cubes with hot water. Add celery and onion mixture, lemon zest, cooked shrimp and lobster and mix well. Run fish under cold water and pat dry. Spread an equal amount of stuffing on each piece of fish and roll up jelly-roll-style. Place stuffed sole in a roasting pan seam-side down. Cover roasting pan and bake for 30 minutes.

SAUCE

2 tbs. butter
2 tbs. finely chopped shallots
1/4 cup dry white wine
1 tbs. fresh lemon juice

1/2 cup fish stock
1 tbs. cornstarch
1 tbs. low-fat plain yogurt

In a small skillet, melt butter over medium heat. Add shallots and sauté for 3-4 minutes or until soft. Add wine and lemon juice. Combine fish broth and cornstarch in a small bowl; mix well. Add cornstarch mixture to skillet, stir continuously and cook until thickened. Remove from heat.

Pour sauce over stuffed sole. Garnish with fresh chopped chives, whole chives and lemon slices.

SWORDFISH WITH GARLIC AND FENNEL

Servings: 4

This is a magnificent dish even for the most selective seafood lover. Garlic, fennel and lemon blend together very nicely for an interesting flavor. Use a mortar and pestle to grind the fennel.

2 lb. swordfish
6 tbs. olive oil
8 cloves garlic, thinly sliced
8 tbs. fresh lemon juice
$1/2$ tsp. ground fennel seeds
fresh cilantro or basil sprigs for garnish

Rinse fish under cold running water and pat dry. Divide fish into 4 equal pieces. Heat 2 tbs. of the olive oil in a 10- or 12-inch nonstick skillet. Cook over medium heat, 2 pieces at a time, for 4 to 5 minutes on each side. Do not overcook fish.

While fish is cooking, heat remaining 4 tbs. olive oil in a small skillet. Add garlic, lemon juice and fennel. Sauté over medium heat for 5 minutes. Place cooked fish on warm individual serving plates. Cover fish with equal portions of garlic-lemon sauce. Garnish with cilantro or basil sprigs.

PAN-FRIED SWORDFISH WITH GARLIC SALSA

Servings: 2

This is simple to prepare, spicy and satisfying. The salsa gives this dish a vibrant presentation. For an alternative, substitute fresh sea bass, tuna or bluefish.

2 swordfish steaks, 8 oz. each
1 tbs. olive oil
1/4 tsp. freshly ground pepper
1/2 cup *Garlic Salsa*, page 17
fresh parsley sprigs for garnish

Rinse fish under cold running water and pat dry. Heat olive oil over medium heat in a nonstick skillet and add pepper. Place fish in skillet and cook for 4 minutes. Turn fish over and spread a layer of *Garlic Salsa* on cooked side. Cover skillet and cook on medium-low heat for 4 more minutes. Transfer fish to serving plates. Serve with remaining salsa on the side for dipping. Garnish with parsley sprigs.

BAKED MACKEREL

You should only cook fresh fish. Always insist on smelling the fish and don't purchase fish that has a strong fishy odor. Fresh mackerel should have shiny skin, firm and moist flesh and a mild ocean odor.

2 tbs. olive or vegetable oil
8 cloves garlic, minced or pressed
2 cans (14.5 oz. each) diced stewed
   tomatoes, with juice
2 medium zucchini, sliced into
   1/4-inch rounds
1/2 lb. mushrooms, thinly sliced

1/2 tsp. dried marjoram
1/2 tsp. dried oregano
1/2 tsp. dried basil
1/2 tsp. chili powder
1/4 tsp. ground cumin
2 lb. mackerel fillets, or bluefish,
   rainbow trout, lake trout or whitefish

Heat oven to 400°. Heat oil in a small saucepan over medium-low heat. Add garlic and sauté for 4 minutes. Set aside and allow to cool. In a large bowl, combine garlic with remaining ingredients, except fish, and mix thoroughly. Rinse fish under cold running water and pat dry. Place fish in an ovenproof baking dish and cover with garlic-tomato sauce. Bake uncovered for 30 minutes.

SPICY TUNA STEAKS

A nonstick grilling rack designed for cooking on an outdoor barbecue is the perfect solution for keeping fish and other delicate foods from sticking, burning and falling apart. These are delicious served with roasted vegetables.

1/4 cup vegetable or olive oil
6 cloves garlic, minced or pressed
3 tbs. low-sodium soy sauce
1/4 tsp. dry mustard
3 tbs. fresh lemon juice
1/2 tsp. freshly ground pepper
2 lb. tuna steaks
1 lemon, cut into wedges

In a medium bowl, combine oil, garlic, soy sauce, mustard, lemon juice and pepper. Mix well. Rinse fish under cold running water and pat dry. Place fish in a shallow bowl and cover with marinade. Refrigerate for 1 hour. Cook fish under a preheated broiler for 5 to 7 minutes on each side, or until opaque, or grill fish on an outdoor barbecue. Pour sauce over fish and serve with lemon wedges.

SKEWERED TUNA WITH GARLIC MARINADE

Servings: 4

Cubes of tuna are infused with a garlic marinade and accompanied by fresh vegetables. You'll find this satisfying and enormously flavorful. Serve with a garden salad.

12 oz. *Basic Garlic Salad Dressing and Marinade*, page 47
2 medium onions
2 medium green bell peppers
1 lb. tuna
16 fresh mushrooms, whole
16 cherry tomatoes
lemon wedges

Prepare marinade, tripling all ingredients. Cut onions into quarters and separate layers. Cut peppers into 1-inch pieces. Rinse fish under cold running water and pat dry. Cut fish into 1-inch cubes, and place in a shallow bowl with onions, peppers, mushrooms and tomatoes. Pour marinade over fish and vegetables. Cover bowl and refrigerate for 3 hours, or overnight.

Alternately thread fish, onions, peppers, mushrooms and tomatoes onto 6 to 8 stainless steel or presoaked bamboo skewers. Place on a hot grill or under a preheated broiler for 8 minutes. Baste with marinade and turn once. Serve with lemon wedges.

BROILED HADDOCK WITH GARLIC AND BASIL

Servings: 4

Almost any delicate white fish such as catfish or flounder will substitute nicely.

2 lb. haddock or cod fillets
1/4 cup olive oil
1/4 cup seasoned breadcrumbs
1/4 tsp. freshly ground pepper
1/4 tsp. paprika
2 cloves garlic, minced or pressed
1/2 tsp. dried basil
1 lemon, cut into wedges

Rinse fish under cold running water and pat dry. Place fish in a metal ovenproof baking pan and coat all sides with 2 tbs. of the olive oil. Cover top of fish with a thin layer of breadcrumbs. Season with pepper and sprinkle with paprika. Broil fish under a preheated broiler for 8 to 10 minutes, or until fish is opaque.

While fish is cooking, heat 2 tbs. olive oil in a small saucepan. Add garlic and basil. Sauté for 2 minutes over medium heat. Pour garlic-basil mixture over fish on individual serving plates. Serve with lemon wedges.

BAKED COD

You can replace the cod with halibut, red snapper, flounder or haddock. Find a good fish market where you're sure the fish is always fresh and properly cleaned.

4 cod steaks, 8 oz. each
2 tsp. dried lemon peel
1 cup breadcrumbs
1 cup skim milk
1/4 tsp. vegetable or olive oil
2 tbs. fresh lemon juice
1 tsp. minced fresh tarragon, or 1/2 tsp. dried
2 cloves garlic, minced or pressed
2 tbs. *Garlic Herb Butter*, page 23

Heat oven to 400°. Rinse fish under cold running water and pat dry. In a shallow bowl, mix together lemon peel and breadcrumbs. Pour milk in another shallow bowl and coat all sides of fish with milk. Dredge fish with breadcrumbs and place in a lightly oiled ovenproof baking dish. Drizzle with lemon juice and sprinkle with tarragon and garlic. Dot with *Garlic Herb Butter*. Bake for 8 to 10 minutes, or until fish is just opaque.

HALIBUT WITH GARLICKY
SUN-DRIED TOMATO PESTO

Servings: 4

Refrigerate the extra pesto and use it as a dipping sauce for calzones, or toss with fresh pasta. Start with dry-packed sun-dried tomatoes.

2 cloves garlic
1/4 cup chopped sun-dried tomatoes, reconstituted
1/4 cup chopped fresh tomatoes
1 cup fresh basil leaves
1/2 cup olive oil
1/4 cup pine nuts or chopped walnuts

1/8 tsp. freshly ground pepper
1/4 cup freshly grated Parmesan cheese
4 halibut steaks, 8 oz. each, 1 inch thick
1/2 tsp. butter, room temperature
fresh parsley or cilantro sprigs for garnish

Heat oven to 475°. Make pesto: combine garlic, sun-dried tomatoes, fresh tomatoes, basil, olive oil, nuts and pepper in a blender or food processor. Puree for 15 to 20 seconds, until a paste forms. Pour into a bowl and mix in Parmesan cheese. Set aside.

Rinse fish under cold running water and pat dry; place in 1 large or 4 individual lightly buttered dishes. Spread a layer of pesto over each piece of fish. Cover with aluminum foil or parchment paper. Bake for 20 minutes. Garnish with fresh parsley or cilantro sprigs.

PARCHMENT SALMON WITH ROASTED GARLIC

Parchment paper is absolutely wonderful for cooking seafood. This is an exciting and delicious recipe to prepare and serve. Serve with a crisp green salad and some crusty bread.

1 bulb garlic, roasted (see page 50)
4 salmon steaks, 4-6 oz. each
4 oz. cream cheese
1 medium-sized firm tomato, chopped
3 tbs. chopped fresh basil
$\frac{1}{2}$ tsp. ground dill weed
$\frac{1}{2}$ tsp. freshly ground pepper
1 tbs. olive oil
2 tbs. freshly grated Parmesan cheese
2 tbs. fresh lemon juice
8 lemon wedges

Heat oven to 400°. Squeeze pulp from roasted garlic cloves and set aside. Rinse fish under cold running water and pat dry. In a medium bowl, combine garlic, cream cheese, tomato, basil, dill and pepper. Mix thoroughly until a paste forms.

Lay out four 15-x-18-inch sheets of parchment paper. Brush entire surface of one side of each sheet with olive oil. Fold parchment paper sheets in half so oiled sides are facing each other. Unfold and sprinkle one side of each sheet with Parmesan cheese. Place 1 salmon steak on top of cheese next to fold. Spread equal portions of garlic-cream cheese mixture on each piece of salmon. Drizzle with lemon juice. Fold and tightly seal each packet by overlapping small ¼-inch folds along 3 sides, or a series of long, thin folds.

Place packets on baking sheets and bake for 20 minutes. Transfer packets to individual serving plates, allowing guests to open packets at the table. Serve with lemon wedges.

ORIENTAL SALMON

I prefer to cook this dish in a wok or stir-fry pan because of its generous size and sloping sides, but you can also use a large 12-inch or 14-inch skillet.

1/2 cup water
1/4 cup hoisin sauce
3 tbs. honey
1 tbs. finely chopped Chinese parsley
1 tbs. minced fresh ginger
1 tbs. brown sugar
1 tbs. white wine vinegar
2 tsp. cornstarch
4 cloves garlic, pressed or minced
3/4 lb. salmon, skinned and cut into 1-inch chunks
1/2 cup diced red bell pepper
1/2 lb. snap peas
1/4 cup frozen green peas, thawed
1/4 tsp. crushed red pepper flakes
2 tbs. canola oil
cooked thin fresh Chinese egg noodles

Combine water, hoisin sauce, honey, Chinese parsley, fresh ginger, sugar, vinegar and cornstarch in a small bowl and set aside.

Heat oil in a wok or stir-fry pan over medium heat. Add garlic and stir-fry for 30 seconds. Add salmon chunks and stir-fry for 2 to 3 minutes. Remove salmon from pan and set aside. Add snap peas, red pepper and green peas to pan and stir-fry for 2 minutes. Add cornstarch mixture and increase heat to medium-high. Bring to a boil. Return salmon to pan and heat through. Sprinkle with crushed red pepper flakes and serve over noodles.

BAKED SALMON WITH SLICED GARLIC

Servings: 4

My dad, an avid salt water fisherman and fabulous cook, once told me that the secret to great-tasting salmon is simple. Just be sure it's fresh and cook it with lots of garlic. Add a garden salad and fresh rolls. Absolutely perfect!

2 lb. salmon
1/3 cup olive oil
4 cloves garlic, cut into 1/4-inch slices
1/4 tsp. dried basil
1/4 tsp. dried parsley
1/4 tsp. freshly ground pepper

Heat oven to 375°. Rinse fish under cold running water and pat dry. Cut fish into 4 equal pieces and place in a shallow stainless steel or ceramic baking dish. Liberally coat all sides of fish with some of the olive oil. Do not allow fish pieces to overlap. Pour remaining olive oil over fish. Cover top layers of fish with garlic slices. Sprinkle with basil, parsley and pepper. Bake uncovered for 20 minutes.

POULTRY

STUFFED CHICKEN BREASTS WITH ROASTED GARLIC SAUCE

A unique wild rice and fig stuffing makes these chicken breasts special. You can substitute long-grain rice for half of the wild rice to help keep the food cost in control and still create a distinctive wild rice flavor. The Roasted Garlic Sauce *is also wonderful over salmon, swordfish or sliced turkey.*

STUFFING

3 cups chicken broth
1 cup uncooked wild rice
1 tbs. butter
1 cup chopped onion
½ cup finely chopped celery
2 cloves garlic, pressed or minced
3 slices prosciutto, chopped

½ cup chopped dried figs
1 tsp. dried thyme
1 tsp. dried parsley flakes
¼ tsp. salt
¼ tsp. black pepper
¼ tsp. paprika

4 chicken breast halves, skinless and boneless, 4 oz. each
1 tsp. olive oil

ROASTED GARLIC SAUCE

6 cloves garlic, roasted (see page 50)	1 tsp. cornstarch
½ cup chicken broth	1 tsp. water
¼ cup white wine	½ tsp. dried basil
1 tbs. fresh lemon juice	

Prepare stuffing: Bring chicken broth to a boil in a medium saucepan. Add wild rice; cover, reduce heat, and simmer for 50 to 55 minutes or until tender. Drain and set aside. Melt butter in a large nonstick skillet over medium heat. Add onion and celery and sauté for 5 minutes. Add garlic and prosciutto and sauté for 3 to 4 minutes. Stir in rice, figs, thyme, parsley, salt, pepper and paprika. Remove from heat and set aside.

Cut a horizontal slit through the thickest portion of each chicken breast half to form a pocket. Stuff each pocket with about ¼ cup of the wild rice mixture. Heat olive oil in a nonstick skillet over medium-high heat. Add chicken breasts and sauté for 6 minutes on each side or until cooked. Remove from pan and keep warm.

Remove roasted garlic from its skin and mash. Add mashed garlic to skillet and sauté for 1 minute over medium heat. Add ½ cup chicken broth, wine and lemon juice to skillet. Bring to a boil; cook for 2 minutes. Combine water and cornstarch; mix well. Add to skillet and whisk. Add dried basil, bring to a boil and cook for 1 minute. Return chicken to skillet and cover. Reduce heat to a simmer and cook for 3 minutes. Serve chicken with sauce and extra wild rice.

CHICKEN AND GARLIC STIR-FRY

Servings: 2

This dish is tasty, has beautiful color, is economical — and has little fat. As with most Chinese dishes, prepare all the ingredients before you begin to cook.

1 cup white rice
2 chicken breast halves, skinned and boned
2 tbs. safflower, sunflower or peanut oil
1/4 cup low sodium soy sauce
1/2 tsp. grated fresh ginger
4 large cloves garlic, thinly sliced
3 medium carrots, peeled and cut into thin matchstick strips
4 cups broccoli florets and chopped stems
2 tbs. water

Prepare rice in a steamer or saucepan. Rinse chicken, pat dry and cut into 1-inch cubes. Heat oil over medium-high heat in a large skillet or wok. Add chicken and sauté for 4 to 5 minutes. Reduce heat to medium. Add soy sauce, ginger, garlic, carrots, broccoli and water. Stir, cover and reduce heat to a low simmer for 5 minutes. Remove from skillet and serve over rice.

CHICKEN WITH 30 CLOVES OF GARLIC

Servings: 4

Thirty cloves of garlic, slowly cooked, create a sauce with splendid aromas and a surprisingly subtle garlic flavor.

2½-3 lb. chicken pieces; legs, breasts or thighs
2 tbs. butter
1¼ cups chicken broth
½ cup white wine
½ cup tomato juice
2 tbs. flour

30 cloves garlic
1 bay leaf
1 tsp. dried thyme
¼ tsp. freshly ground pepper
¼ tsp. salt
cooked white rice or pasta

Rinse chicken pieces and pat dry. Heat butter in a large skillet and brown chicken pieces on each side over medium-high heat. Remove chicken from skillet and set aside.

Add chicken broth, wine, tomato juice and flour to skillet. Stir and bring to a quick boil. Reduce heat to low. Add garlic, bay leaf, thyme, pepper, salt and chicken. Cover and simmer for 1 hour and 15 minutes. Remove chicken. Pour sauce through a gravy separator, or skim off fat from top of liquid. Serve chicken on individual serving plates with white rice or pasta and top with sauce.

GARLIC AND OREGANO CHICKEN

Servings: 4

This scrumptious chicken dish is one of my favorites, an outstanding combination of ingredients. I serve it often and it's always a hit. Serve with Garlic Roasted Potatoes, *page 69.*

4 chicken breast halves, skinned and boned
1/2 cup skim milk
1/2 cup seasoned breadcrumbs
2 tbs. olive oil
2 tbs. butter

6 cloves garlic, minced or pressed
2 tbs. dried oregano
1/4 cup dry sherry
1 cup shredded fontina cheese
1 cup diced tomato

Rinse chicken and pat dry. Dip chicken into skim milk. Coat each side with breadcrumbs and shake off excess. Heat olive oil in a skillet and sauté each side of chicken for 10 minutes; set aside.

Melt butter in a small saucepan. Add garlic, oregano and sherry. Mix and set aside. Place chicken breasts on a baking sheet, making sure pieces do not overlap. Spread a layer of cheese over each breast. Cover cheese with a layer of diced tomatoes. Slowly pour oregano mixture over tomatoes, covering each piece of chicken. Place under a preheated broiler for 2 to 3 minutes.

SKEWERED CHICKEN WITH SLICED GARLIC

Servings: 4

I use a stainless steel garlic "mandolin" for slicing the garlic into thin pieces. It's easy to use, reasonably priced and is available at most gourmet shops. Serve these kabobs with white rice and a garden salad.

4 chicken breast halves, skinned and boned
1 cup *Garlicky Vinaigrette*, page 46
1 large green bell pepper
1 large white or red onion
16 cloves garlic
1 large tomato

Rinse chicken, pat dry and cut into 1-inch cubes. Combine chicken and vinaigrette in a large bowl and marinate chicken in the refrigerator for 2 hours. Cut pepper into 1-inch pieces. Cut onion into quarters and separate layers. Peel and slice garlic into thin 1/8-inch slices. Cut tomato into 8 wedges and cut each wedge in half to create 16 pieces. Alternately thread chicken cubes, garlic, pepper, garlic, onion, garlic and tomato pieces onto eight 10-inch metal or presoaked bamboo skewers. Thread slices of garlic between pieces of food. Place skewers in a preheated broiler or on a medium-high grill and cook for 10 to 12 minutes. Turn and brush with marinade occasionally.

CHICKEN PESTO

Serve as a robust lunch or dinner with fresh vegetables and garlic bread. Pesto is wonderful tossed with hot pasta, used as a topping for pizza, and for many other uses.

PESTO
2 cups fresh basil leaves
3 cloves garlic
1 cup olive oil
$\frac{1}{2}$ cup pine nuts or chopped walnuts
$\frac{1}{2}$ tsp. freshly ground pepper
$\frac{1}{2}$ cup freshly grated Parmesan cheese

Combine basil, garlic, olive oil, nuts and pepper in a food processor or blender container. Process for 15 to 20 seconds, or until a paste forms. Pour into a bowl and mix in Parmesan cheese. Set aside.

1 whole chicken, 4-5 lb.
1 clove garlic, thinly sliced
1 tbs. olive oil
¼ tsp. dried thyme
¼ tsp. freshly ground pepper
2 tbs. butter, melted
fresh lettuce

Heat oven to 325°. Remove giblets
from chicken. Rinse chicken and pat dry.
Tuck garlic slices under skin and rub skin
with olive oil. Sprinkle chicken with thyme
and pepper. Place chicken on a rack, breast side
up, in a shallow ovenproof roasting pan.

Bake for 2 to 2½ hours, or until chicken
temperature reaches 180° on an instant-read meat thermometer. Baste with butter and pan drippings every 15 to 20 minutes. Remove from oven and cool.
Discard skin and cut meat into bite-sized pieces. Toss chicken pieces with pesto.
Serve warm or cold on lettuce-lined serving plates.

JOANNE'S CHICKEN AND GARLIC CHILI

My wife Joanne worked diligently with me on testing and developing this special collection of delicious garlic recipes. She is truly a gifted cook. This is her own version of chili. It's the best I've ever had!

1 tbs. olive oil
6 cloves garlic, minced or pressed
2 medium onions, diced
2 medium green bell peppers, diced
2 cans (14.5 oz. each) stewed tomatoes, chopped, with juice
1 can (15.5 oz.) pinto beans, drained
1 can (28 oz.) crushed tomatoes
1 tsp. ground cumin
6 tbs. chili powder
1/3 cup all-purpose flour
1 lb. chicken, cooked and sliced

In a large stockpot, heat olive oil and sauté garlic, onions and green peppers over medium heat until tender. Add remaining ingredients and mix well. Bring to a boil, reduce heat to low, cover and simmer for 1 1/2 hours.

BAKED GARLIC AND HERB CHICKEN BREASTS Servings: 4

This is an ideal mid-week recipe for someone with a busy schedule. Just prepare the dish before you go to work and place the chicken in the oven when you get home, allowing yourself plenty of time to put together a fresh garden salad.

4 chicken breast halves, skinned and boned
1/4 cup olive oil
3 tbs. fresh lemon juice
4 cloves garlic, minced or pressed
2 tbs. minced onion
1 tsp. dried basil
1 tsp. dried thyme
1/2 tsp. freshly ground pepper

Rinse chicken under cold water and pat dry. Combine all ingredients, except chicken, in a bowl and mix thoroughly. Arrange chicken breasts in an ovenproof baking dish in one layer and cover with garlic-herb marinade. Refrigerate for at least 2 hours, or overnight.

Heat oven to 375°. Bake chicken in marinade for 40 minutes.

CRISPY AROMATIC CHICKEN

This savory chicken dish has an irresistible Oriental flavor.

2 chicken breast halves, skinned and boned
1 cup cornstarch
1 cup all-purpose flour
1 cup water
1 egg
1 tsp. baking powder
1 cup plus 1 tbs. canola or peanut oil

1 tbs. minced fresh ginger
3 cloves garlic, minced
4 cups broccoli florets and sliced stems
1 medium red or green bell pepper, cut into 1-inch pieces
1 can (8 oz.) water chestnuts, drained
sauce, follows
steamed white rice

Rinse chicken, pat dry and cut into 1-inch cubes. Combine cornstarch, flour, water, egg and baking powder. Mix thoroughly. Heat 1 cup oil in a wok or large skillet. Dip chicken pieces in batter and sauté in oil for 10 to 12 minutes, or until golden brown on all sides. Set chicken aside and remove oil from skillet.

Heat remaining 1 tbs. oil in skillet. Add ginger and garlic. Stir-fry for 1 minute. Add broccoli, bell pepper and water chestnuts. Stir-fry for 2 minutes. Add sauce and chicken. Stir, cover and cook for 3 to 4 minutes. Serve hot with sauce over steamed white rice.

SAUCE

1 clove garlic, thinly sliced
¼ cup low-sodium soy sauce
½ cup brown sugar, packed
1 medium onion, diced
1 tbs. honey

Combine ingredients in a bowl. Mix thoroughly.

PARCHMENT CHICKEN
WITH ROASTED GARLIC

Parchment paper is ideal for baking chicken. Find it in most supermarkets and specialty kitchen shops. Cleanup is quick and easy. Serve with vegetables or a salad.

1 bulb garlic, roasted (see page 50)
1/4 tsp. dried thyme
1/4 tsp. dried basil
1/4 tsp. dried parsley
1/4 tsp. dried marjoram

4 chicken breast halves, skinned and
  boned
1/2 cup skim milk
1/2 cup seasoned breadcrumbs
3 tbs. olive oil

Heat oven to 375°. Squeeze pulp from roasted garlic cloves and set aside. In a small bowl, combine garlic, thyme, basil, parsley and marjoram. Mix thoroughly. Rinse chicken and pat dry. Pour milk into a shallow dish and dip chicken in milk. Coat with breadcrumbs and shake off excess. Heat olive oil in a skillet and sauté chicken for 2 minutes on each side. Remove from skillet and set aside.

Lay out four 18-x-15-inch sheets parchment paper and fold in half. Unfold and place 1 chicken breast on each sheet next to the fold. Spread 1/4 of the garlic mixture on top of each breast. Fold and tightly seal packets with a series of long, thin folds. Place packets on baking sheets and bake for 30 minutes. Transfer packets to individual serving plates, allowing guests to open packets at the table.

CHICKEN CUTLETS

These are so delicious and such a great crowd-pleaser that a tomato or marinara sauce isn't necessary. The recipe can easily be adapted for smaller or larger quantities. These can be prepared a day in advance. Just reheat in a 325° oven for 10 to 15 minutes.

4 chicken breast halves, skinned and boned
1 cup seasoned breadcrumbs
1/2 tsp. garlic powder
2 tbs. freshly grated Parmesan cheese
1/2 tsp. dried basil
1/4 tsp. freshly ground pepper
1/2 cup olive oil
1 egg, beaten

Rinse chicken under cold running water and pat dry. Fillet each breast into 3 thin cutlets. Tenderize each cutlet with a wooden or metal mallet. In a shallow bowl, combine breadcrumbs, garlic powder, cheese, basil and pepper.

Heat olive oil over medium heat in a large skillet. Start with 3 tbs. olive oil and add more as needed. If cooking in an electric frying pan, set temperature at 350°. Dip cutlets in egg and coat with breadcrumb mixture. Shake off excess. Sauté each piece of chicken for 5 to 6 minutes on each side, or until golden brown. Place cooked cutlets on a paper towel-lined platter to absorb excess oil.

BISTRO GARLIC CHICKEN

Servings: 4

Boneless chicken breasts are stuffed with a spicy blend of minced vegetables and topped with tomato sauce and melted cheese.

8 chicken breast halves, skinned and
  boned
6 cloves garlic, minced or pressed
1/3 cup minced sun-dried tomatoes,
  reconstituted
1/2 cup minced marinated artichoke
  hearts
1/4 cup minced black olives

2 tbs. minced onion
1/4 cup minced green bell pepper
1/2 tsp. dried basil
1/4 tsp. freshly ground pepper
3 cups tomato sauce
1/2 cup shredded fontina cheese
1 tbs. grated Parmesan cheese
chopped fresh parsley for garnish

Heat oven to 375°. Rinse chicken and pat dry. In a medium bowl, combine garlic, sun-dried tomatoes, artichoke hearts, olives, onion, green peppers, basil and pepper. Mix thoroughly.

Place 4 chicken breast halves in an ovenproof casserole. Spread 1/4 of mixture on top of each breast. Cover each breast with another chicken breast. Spoon tomato sauce on top of chicken and sprinkle with fontina and Parmesan cheeses. Bake uncovered for 40 minutes. Garnish with parsley and serve immediately.

CHICKEN FAJITAS

An oval cast iron or anodized aluminum skillet is ideal for preparing fajitas. It heats up quickly, maintains the temperature and creates an interesting presentation.

4 chicken breast halves, skinned and boned
3 cloves garlic, pressed
3 tbs. olive oil
1/4 cup fresh lime juice
1/2 tsp. dried oregano
1/2 tsp. freshly ground pepper
8 corn or flour tortillas
shredded lettuce, refried beans, chopped onions, guacamole, salsa and sour
    cream, optional

Rinse chicken and pat dry. Cut chicken into long strips, about 1/2-inch wide. In a shallow bowl, combine garlic, 2 tbs. olive oil, lime juice, oregano and pepper. Mix well. Add chicken strips, cover and refrigerate for 2 hours or overnight. Turn occasionally in marinade. Heat 1 tbs. olive oil in a preheated skillet. Add chicken and cook over medium-high heat for 1 minute on each side, or until browned and cooked. Serve with warm tortillas and desired fillings.

THE ODD COUPLE

Sautéed chicken chunks and garlicky blueberry dipping sauce are a different and delicious taste treat to serve at your next buffet.

GARLICKY BLUEBERRY DIPPING SAUCE

4 cups blueberries, fresh or frozen, thawed
2 cloves garlic, minced or pressed
3/4 cup brown sugar, packed
1/4 cup sugar
1/4 cup fresh lemon juice
1/2 tsp. lemon peel
1/2 cup balsamic vinegar

Combine all ingredients in a saucepan. Bring to a boil. Reduce heat, cover and simmer for 20 minutes. Cool and serve at room temperature, or refrigerate and serve cold in individual ramekins for dipping *Sautéed Chicken.*

SAUTÉED CHICKEN

4 chicken breast halves, skinned and boned
2 tbs. olive oil
2 cloves garlic, minced or pressed
1 tsp. freshly ground pepper
2 tsp. chopped fresh basil
2 tsp. chopped fresh parsley
lettuce leaves

Rinse chicken and pat dry. Cut into 1-x-2-inch pieces. Heat olive oil in a skillet. Add garlic and sauté for 1 minute. Add chicken and pepper. Sauté for 3 to 4 minutes on each side. Add basil and parsley. Sauté for 5 more minutes, or until thoroughly cooked. Serve on individual plates, or on a large serving platter lined with lettuce leaves along with *Garlicky Blueberry Dipping Sauce.*

ULTIMATE CHICKEN WINGS

Serve these on your next buffet, or take them on a picnic. They're good hot or cold.

2 lb. chicken wings, about 12
1 tbs. vegetable or olive oil
4 cloves garlic, minced or pressed
$1/2$ cup brown sugar, packed
$1/2$ tsp. ground ginger
1 tbs. honey
$1/4$ cup low-sodium soy sauce
1 medium onion, diced

Remove excess skin from chicken wings. Rinse and pat dry. Heat olive oil in a skillet and sauté chicken wings for 12 minutes over medium heat. Add more oil if needed. Thoroughly combine garlic, brown sugar, ginger, honey, soy sauce and onion in a large bowl. Marinate wings in mixture for 2 hours or overnight in the refrigerator.

Heat oven to 450°. Place chicken wings in a shallow baking pan with $3/4$ of the marinade. Bake wings for 35 minutes. Baste occasionally with remaining marinade. Broil for 2 minutes.

LEMON GARLIC CHICKEN

This robust dish is for the more adventuresome.

2 chicken breast halves, skinned and
  boned
1 egg
2 tbs. milk
1/2 cup flour
1 tbs. olive oil
1 cup chicken broth

1/4 cup dry sherry
juice of 1/2 lemon
1 tbs. chopped garlic
2 tbs. chopped fresh basil
8 oz. dried bow tie pasta
1/4 tsp. freshly ground pepper, optional
2 tbs. freshly grated Parmesan cheese

Rinse chicken and pat dry. Combine egg and milk in a shallow bowl. Dip chicken in egg-milk mixture. Coat with flour and shake off excess. Heat olive oil in a skillet and sauté chicken for 5 minutes on each side. Add chicken broth, sherry, lemon juice and garlic. Bring to a boil. Cover skillet, reduce heat and simmer for 20 minutes. Add basil during last 5 minutes of cooking.

While chicken is cooking, cook pasta according to package instructions. Drain pasta. Place cooked chicken on a serving plate with pasta and pour lemon-garlic sauce over all. Sprinkle with pepper and Parmesan cheese.

LEMON DIJON AND GARLIC CHICKEN

Servings: 4

A treat for mustard lovers! Serve with Garlic Roasted Potatoes, *page 69, and a garden salad.*

2 tbs. fresh lemon juice
2 tbs. Dijon mustard
3 cloves garlic, minced or pressed
2 tbs. vegetable or olive oil
1/4 cup low-sodium soy sauce
1/4 tsp. freshly ground pepper
4 chicken breast halves, skinned and boned

In a medium bowl, combine lemon juice, mustard, garlic, oil, soy sauce and pepper. Mix thoroughly. Rinse chicken and pat dry. Place chicken in an ovenproof casserole. Pour marinade over chicken, cover casserole and refrigerate for 2 hours, or overnight.

Heat oven to 350°. Bake covered casserole for 30 minutes. Remove cover and bake for 30 more minutes, basting occasionally.

MEATS

LEMON GARLIC VEAL

The garlic is the key to this delicious sauce. Serve with linguine.

1 large egg
½ lb. veal cutlets
¼ cup flour
⅛ tsp. freshly ground pepper
¼ cup butter
2 tbs. olive oil
4 cloves garlic, thinly sliced
2 tbs. fresh lemon juice
1 tbs. minced fresh basil

Beat egg in a shallow bowl. Cut and pound veal into thin pieces. Dip veal in egg and dredge in flour. Season both sides of veal with pepper.

Melt 2 tbs. of the butter in a skillet. Sauté veal over medium heat on each side for 2 to 3 minutes, or until brown. While veal is cooking, heat 2 tbs. olive oil and remaining 2 tbs. butter in a small skillet. Add garlic, lemon juice and basil. Sauté over medium heat for 4 minutes. Place cooked veal on 2 individual warm serving plates. Cover each plate of veal with half the sauce and serve.

VEAL PARMIGIANA

Thin slices of turkey or chicken breast will substitute nicely for the veal.

1 large egg
2 tbs. freshly grated Parmesan cheese
1/4 tsp. garlic powder
1 cup seasoned breadcrumbs
1 lb. veal cutlets, about 1/3-inch thick

2 tbs. olive oil
2 tbs. butter
2 cloves garlic, minced or pressed
2 cups tomato sauce
1/2 cup shredded mozzarella cheese

Heat oven to 350°. Beat egg in a shallow bowl. Add 1 tbs. of the Parmesan cheese and garlic powder to breadcrumbs and mix. Dip cutlets in egg and coat with breadcrumbs. Shake off excess.

Heat olive oil and butter in a large skillet. Add garlic and sauté for 1 minute. Add cutlets and sauté for 2 to 3 minutes on each side, or until golden brown. Spread 3/4 cup tomato sauce in a baking dish. Arrange cutlets in a single layer over sauce and cover with mozzarella cheese. Spread remaining sauce over mozzarella and sprinkle with remaining Parmesan cheese. Bake covered for 20 minutes. Remove lid and bake for 5 more minutes.

VARIATION

Place a thin slice of prosciutto on each cutlet and cover with cheese and sauce.

ROAST PORK WITH GARLIC SLICES

To reduce the garlic odor from your breath, try eating 2 or 3 sprigs of flat-leaf (Italian) parsley after a meal. It doesn't totally eliminate the odor, but it helps.

1 pork loin, about 4-5 lb., boned
5 cloves garlic, cut in half
1 tbs. olive oil
1/4 tsp. dried thyme
1/4 tsp. dried rosemary
1/4 tsp. dried sage
1/4 tsp. freshly ground pepper
1 medium onion, thinly sliced
8-10 small red-skinned potatoes, quartered

Heat oven to 350°. Cut garlic cloves in half. Make 10 random slits in roast. Insert a piece of garlic into each slit. Rub roast with olive oil and season with thyme, rosemary, sage and pepper. Place pork loin in a roasting pan; surround with onion slices and potatoes. Bake for 2 hours, or until pork reaches 160° on an instant-read meat thermometer. Remove meat and potatoes from roasting pan. Allow roast to rest for at least 10 minutes before carving.

SKEWERED PORK STRIPS

To prevent the bamboo skewers from burning on the grill or in the broiler, soak them in cold water for 1 hour. Serve with steamed white rice or over fresh spinach.

1 lb. pork loin
2 tbs. hot water
$1/2$ cup brown sugar, packed
2 cloves garlic, minced or pressed
2 tbs. low-sodium soy sauce
1 tbs. oyster sauce
2 tbs. dry sherry
1 tsp. sesame oil

Cut pork into $1\,1/2$-x-6-inch strips. Combine hot water with brown sugar in a medium stainless steel bowl. Stir for about 2 minutes, or until brown sugar has dissolved. Add remaining ingredients, except meat, and mix thoroughly. Add pork strips and marinate for 4 hours, or overnight, in the refrigerator. Mix occasionally.

Thread pork strips on 10-inch bamboo skewers and cook on a grill or under a broiler for 8 to 10 minutes. Turn and baste frequently with remaining marinade.

STUFFED PORK ROAST
WITH RED PEPPER SAUCE

This beautifully presented main dish takes center stage on any holiday or special occasion table. For a new tradition, it's a great alternative to turkey on Thanksgiving Day.

1 boneless pork loin roast, about
   2-2½ lb.
2 tbs. butter
¼ cup finely chopped onions
¼ cup finely chopped celery
3 tbs. toasted pine nuts
3 cups dry bread cubes
¾ cup hot water
½ tsp. dried thyme
½ tsp. dried sage
¼ tsp. dried marjoram

½-¾ tsp. rubbed sage
salt and pepper to taste
4 red bell peppers, cut into ¼-inch
   strips
fresh rosemary sprigs for garnish
3 medium onions, quartered and layers
   separated
10 cloves garlic, peeled
2 celery stalks, cut into thirds
½ cup water

Toast pine nuts: Place nuts in a small nonstick skillet and cook over medium heat for 2 to 3 minutes or until nuts turn brown. Stir frequently.

Heat oven to 350°. In a large skillet, melt butter and sauté onion and celery until onion is soft. In a medium bowl, combine bread cubes and water. Mix well. Add onion and celery mixture, thyme, sage and marjoram. Mix well. Cut a pocket in pork loin and fill with stuffing. Tie loin in three places to secure. Place meat in a roasting pan fat-side up and rub with salt, pepper and sage. Scatter peppers, onions and garlic around meat. Roast for 1 to 1½ hours, or until the internal temperature reaches 160°. Remove roast from oven and let rest for 10 minutes. Discard celery stalks.

Warm red pepper sauce over medium heat. Pour about ½ cup of sauce onto a warm serving platter. Slice pork and place on top of sauce. Arrange peppers, onions and garlic on platter with pork. Garnish with fresh rosemary sprigs. Serve with remaining warmed red pepper sauce.

RED PEPPER SAUCE

2 medium red bell peppers, roasted
  (see page 51)
1 tbs. extra virgin olive oil

1 clove garlic
salt and pepper to taste

Puree skinned peppers, olive oil and garlic with a food processor or blender. Season with salt and pepper. Serve warm.

GARLIC-FLAVORED PORK CHOPS

This basic dish is easy to prepare, flavorful and very succulent.

1/4 cup skim milk
1/4 cup seasoned breadcrumbs
1/4 tsp. garlic powder
1 tbs. freshly grated Parmesan cheese
1 tbs. chopped fresh parsley
1/4 tsp. dried basil
1/4 tsp. freshly ground pepper
4 pork chops, 1/2-inch thick
1/4 cup olive oil

Pour milk into a shallow dish. In another shallow dish, combine breadcrumbs, garlic powder, Parmesan cheese, parsley, basil and pepper. Mix well. Dip chops into milk, coat with breadcrumb mixture and shake off excess. Heat olive oil in a skillet and sauté chops gently over medium heat for 5 to 6 minutes on each side, or until golden brown. Serve with mashed potatoes.

GARLIC-FLAVORED LAMB KABOBS

The distinctive flavors of garlic and lamb cook together beautifully. This makes an ideal meal for an informal setting on a warm summer night. Serve with Hummus, *page 18,* Taboulleh, *page 42, and lots of small pita bread wedges.*

2 lb. lean lamb
16 oz. *Garlicky Vinaigrette*, page 46
1 tsp. dried mint, or 1 tbs. minced fresh
1 medium eggplant
2 medium red bell peppers
6 cloves garlic

Cut lamb into 1-inch cubes. Prepare *Garlicky Vinaigrette* for marinade, doubling all ingredients. Combine marinade with mint and mix well. Place cubes of lamb in a shallow bowl with marinade. Cover and refrigerate for 2 hours, or overnight. Turn occasionally in marinade. Peel eggplant and cut into 1-inch cubes. Cut peppers into 1-inch pieces. Peel and slice garlic cloves into 1/4-inch slices. Alternately thread lamb, garlic, eggplant and peppers onto presoaked bamboo skewers. Place on a medium-hot grill or under a broiler for 15 minutes. Baste with marinade and turn frequently. Serve with rice and a garden salad.

ROASTED LAMB

Servings: 6

A V-shaped, heavy gauge roasting rack with adjustable sides will prevent the lamb from absorbing excess fat and works well for cooling cooked meats. Sautéed vegetables and rice make a nice accompaniment.

4 lb. leg of lamb, bone removed, tied
3 cloves garlic, pressed
¼ cup olive oil
1 tbs. minced fresh rosemary, or 1 tsp. crushed dried
¼ tsp. dried dill weed
¼ tsp. freshly ground pepper

Heat oven to 400°. In a small bowl, combine garlic, olive oil, rosemary, dill weed and pepper. Mix well. Place lamb in a deep pan and cover with marinade. Place a sheet of foil over lamb and refrigerate for 4 hours, or overnight. Baste occasionally with marinade. Place lamb on a V-shaped rack in a roasting pan and roast for 48 to 50 minutes, or until lamb reaches 155° on an instant-read meat thermometer. Remove from oven and cool for 10 minutes. Slice lamb in thin pieces to serve.

LAMB CHOPS

The spicy garlic butter adds a delicious flavor to the lamb chops. It goes well with a fresh sliced tomato salad, or serve over a nutritious bed of lentils.

4 rib or loin lamb chops, about 1¼ inches thick
4 cloves garlic, minced or pressed
½ tsp. ground dried rosemary
½ cup *Garlic Herb Butter*, page 23
freshly ground pepper, optional

Trim excess fat from lamb chops. Place chops in a shallow dish and cover with garlic and rosemary. Refrigerate for 2 hours, or overnight.

Place chops under a broiler and cook for about 4 to 5 minutes on each side. Use tongs to turn meat over; do not pierce with a fork. Continue to broil until chops are done, about 4 to 5 minutes. Remove chops from broiler. Serve garlic-and-rosemary-side up. Top with *Garlic Herb Butter*, season with pepper and serve immediately on warm plates.

BEEF AND GARLIC STIR-FRY

Quick, easy and delicious. A delightful blend of vegetables and beef creates this exciting Chinese-style dish. Serve over white rice.

2 tsp. cornstarch
3 tbs. low-sodium soy sauce
1/4 cup water
1/2 tsp. sugar
1/2 tsp. freshly ground pepper
3 tbs. canola, peanut or vegetable oil
5 cloves garlic, minced or pressed
1 lb. flank steak, thinly sliced
2 red bell peppers, sliced into matchstick strips
2 cups thinly sliced celery

In a small bowl, combine cornstarch, soy sauce, water, sugar and pepper. Set aside. Heat 2 tbs. oil in a large skillet or wok over medium-high heat. Add garlic and sauté for 20 seconds. Add beef and sauté for 3 to 4 minutes. Remove beef and set aside. Heat remaining oil in skillet. Add bell peppers and celery. Stir-fry for 3 minutes. Pour in soy sauce mixture. Add beef and stir-fry all ingredients for 2 minutes.

GARLIC MEAT LOAF

A garlic lover's delight! Serve hot or cold. Slice leftover meat loaf for fabulous sandwiches.

2 lb. ground chuck
2 cups breadcrumbs
1 egg, beaten
1/2 cup milk
2 medium onions, minced
2 cloves garlic, minced or pressed
1/4 cup minced celery
1/4 cup minced red or green bell
   peppers

2 tsp. Worcestershire sauce
1 tsp. dry mustard
2 tsp. minced fresh parsley
1/2 tsp. freshly ground pepper
1/4 tsp. dried oregano
8-9 cloves garlic, thinly sliced

Heat oven to 350°. In a large bowl, combine all ingredients except garlic slices. Using clean hands, mix thoroughly. Pat meat mixture evenly into a meat loaf pan. Completely cover top of meat loaf with a layer of garlic slices. Bake for 1 hour and 15 minutes.

BEEF FAJITAS

This dish is fun and easy to prepare. Serve these sizzling and spicy beef strips at the table or right from the skillet. They make a spectacular presentation for a party setting.

1 lb. flank steak
2 cloves garlic, pressed
1/2 cup olive oil
1 tbs. fresh lime juice
1/4 tsp. ground cumin
1 tsp. chili powder
1 tsp. dried oregano

1/4 tsp. freshly ground pepper
8 corn or flour tortillas
sliced avocado, chopped red onion,
    refried beans, diced tomatoes,
    shredded lettuce and sliced jalapeño
    peppers for filling

Cut flank steak into 1/4-inch-thick slices across the grain. In a small bowl, combine garlic, olive oil, lime juice, cumin, chili powder, oregano and pepper. Mix well. Add meat strips, cover and refrigerate for 6 hours, or overnight. Heat a fajita pan or large skillet. Add marinated meat with marinade and cook on medium-high heat for 1 to 1 1/2 minutes on each side, or until meat is cooked through. Serve with warmed tortillas and desired fillings.

LONDON BROIL

Fresh garlic enhances the meat for a great-tasting and tender steak. Serve it with rice and salad.

1 London broil or flank steak, about 1 1/2 lb.
2 cloves garlic, cut in half
2 tsp. vegetable or olive oil
1/4 tsp. freshly ground pepper

Rub all sides of steak with garlic. Coat steak with oil and sprinkle with pepper. Preheat the broiler for 10 minutes. Place steak on a lightly greased rack 4 inches from heat. Cook steak for 6 to 7 minutes on each side. To serve, carve meat into thin slices diagonally across the grain.

SLOPPY GARLICKY BURGERS

Servings: 4-6

In 1979, the first garlic festival in Gilroy, California, attracted about 15,000 people. Recent attendance has reached over 130,000 and the crowd continues to grow each year.

¼ cup bulghur wheat
½ cup water
1 lb. ground chuck
1 medium onion, minced
4 cloves garlic, minced or pressed
½ cup ketchup
½ tsp. dried basil
½ tsp. freshly ground pepper
¼ tsp. chili powder
pita bread or buns

Soak bulghur wheat in water for 1 hour. Sauté meat and onions in a nonstick skillet until brown, about 5 to 6 minutes. Drain. Drain water from bulghur. Add bulghur, garlic, ketchup, basil, pepper and chili powder to meat. Mix thoroughly and cook over low heat for 5 minutes. Stir occasionally. Serve in sliced pita pockets or on buns.

BROILED STEAK WITH GARLIC SAUCE

Servings: 4

This garlic-flavored beef dish is really tender and has a wonderful flavor. It's also perfect for the backyard grill.

3 tbs. butter
2 cloves garlic, minced or pressed
1 tbs. olive or vegetable oil
$\frac{1}{2}$ tsp. dried oregano
$\frac{1}{2}$ tsp. ground dried rosemary
$\frac{1}{4}$ tsp. freshly ground pepper
1 T-bone or porterhouse steak, 1 inch thick, about 2 lb.

Melt butter in a small saucepan. Combine melted butter with garlic, oil, oregano, rosemary and pepper. Trim excess fat from steak. Preheat the broiler for 10 minutes. Place steak on a lightly greased broiler rack set 4 inches from heat. Broil steak on each side for 5 minutes. Spread layer of garlic sauce on top of steak. Return to broiler and cook until done. To test, insert an instant-read meat thermometer into center of steak. Thermometer should read 130° for rare, 140° for medium and 160° for well done. Remove steak from broiler and serve immediately on warm serving plates.

FOREVER FAVORITE GARLICKY BEEF STEW

Servings: 8

A relaxing and easy dish to prepare that's hearty and satisfying, this stew is an ideal main course for a fall picnic or a winter buffet.

1 lb. lean beef, cut into 1-inch cubes
1/4 cup flour
1/4 cup vegetable or olive oil
3/4 cup celery, cut into 3/4-inch pieces
1 large onion, chopped
4 cups water
1 pkg. dry onion soup mix
1/4 cup red wine
12 cloves garlic, peeled
1/2 tsp. dried thyme
1/2 tsp. pepper

1/8 tsp. ground dried sage
1/4 tsp. dried marjoram
1/4 tsp. salt
2 medium carrots, cut into 1/4-inch slices
1 red or green bell pepper, cut into 1-inch pieces
1 cup eggplant, peeled and cut into 1-inch cubes
4 small new potatoes, peeled and cut into 1-inch cubes

Coat beef with flour and set aside. Heat 2 tbs. oil in a large skillet and brown beef over medium heat for 10 to 12 minutes. Drain off fat and set aside. Heat 2 tbs. oil in a large pot or flameproof casserole. Add celery and onion and sauté for 3 minutes over medium heat. Add water and bring to a boil. Reduce heat; add soup mix, wine, garlic, spices and beef. Mix thoroughly and simmer for 1 hour and 15 minutes. Add remaining ingredients and simmer for 1 hour, or until vegetables are tender.

BEEF TENDERLOIN WITH
ROASTED GARLIC CRUST AND ROASTED ONIONS

Servings: 6

This recipe comes together very easily and produces perfect results. The roasted garlic crust is the perfect complement to the beef tenderloin. It's an impressive centerpiece for a truly memorable meal.

1 large bulb garlic, roasted and cooled (see page 50)
3 tbs. olive oil
1/8 tsp. dried basil
1/8 tsp. dried thyme
1/4 cup prepared cream-style horseradish
1/4 tsp. salt
freshly ground pepper to taste
6 medium-sized sweet white onions
olive oil for brushing onions
3 lbs. beef tenderloin

Separate roasted garlic cloves and squeeze out garlic. Place garlic in a food processor workbowl with 2 tbs. of the olive oil, basil, thyme, horseradish, salt and pepper to taste. Puree until smooth.

Trim fat from beef. Coat all sides evenly with horseradish-garlic mixture. Place in a large roasting pan, cover and refrigerate for 6 to 8 hours.

Heat oven to 400°. Place beef on a roasting rack in a large roasting pan. Cut onions in half crosswise. Do not peel. Make a small slit on each side of each onion half. Brush cut sides of onions with remaining olive oil. Place onions cut-side down in roasting pan around rack. Roast for 40 minutes or until an instant-read thermometer reads 145° for medium-rare or 160° for medium. Remove from oven; cover with an aluminum foil tent and let rest for 10 minutes. Slice beef and serve with onions. You can remove onion skins if you prefer.

SIRLOIN KABOBS

If you serve kabobs often, you can find wonderful metal skewers with decorated handles in many kitchen shops. I like to serve this succulent dish as a main course with String Bean and Garlic Mix, *page 62, and rice.*

1/2 cup dry red wine
3 cloves garlic, minced or pressed
2 tbs. vegetable oil
1 tbs. grated fresh ginger
2 tbs. low sodium soy sauce
1/2 tsp. dried oregano

1/2 tsp. dried thyme
1/4 tsp. freshly ground pepper
1 lb. sirloin, cut into 1-x-1 1/2-inch cubes
18 mushroom caps
1 medium onion

In a large bowl, combine wine, garlic, oil, ginger, soy sauce, oregano, thyme and pepper. Mix well. Add meat and mushrooms and marinate in the refrigerator for at least 2 hours, or overnight. Cut onion into quarters and separate layers. Alternately thread meat, onion slices and mushroom caps onto presoaked bamboo skewers or metal skewers. Grill or broil 3 inches from heat for 15 minutes. Turn and baste occasionally with remaining marinade while cooking.

INDEX

Serve Creative, Easy, Nutritious Meals with nitty gritty® Cookbooks

100 Dynamite Desserts
The 9 x 13 Pan Cookbook
The Barbecue Cookbook
Beer and Good Food
The Best Bagels are Made at Home
The Best Pizza is Made at Home
The Big Book of Bread Machine
   Recipes
Bread Baking
Bread Machine Cookbook
Bread Machine Cookbook II
Bread Machine Cookbook III
Bread Machine Cookbook IV
Bread Machine Cookbook V
Bread Machine Cookbook VI
Cappuccino/Espresso
Casseroles
The Coffee Book
Convection Oven Cookery
The Cook-Ahead Cookbook
Cooking for 1 or 2
Cooking in Clay
Cooking in Porcelain

Cooking on the Indoor Grill
Cooking with Chile Peppers
Cooking with Grains
Cooking with Your Kids
The Dehydrator Cookbook
Edible Pockets for Every Meal
Extra-Special Crockery Pot Recipes
Fabulous Fiber Cookery
Fondue and Hot Dips
Fresh Vegetables
From Freezer, 'Fridge and Pantry
From Your Ice Cream Maker
The Garlic Cookbook
Gourmet Gifts
Healthy Cooking on the Run
Healthy Snacks for Kids
The Juicer Book
The Juicer Book II
Lowfat American Favorites
New International Fondue Cookbook
No Salt, No Sugar, No Fat
One-Dish Meals
The Pasta Machine Cookbook

Pinch of Time: Meals in Less than 30
   Minutes
Quick and Easy Pasta Recipes
Recipes for the Loaf Pan
Recipes for the Pressure Cooker
Recipes for Yogurt Cheese
Risottos, Paellas, and other Rice
   Specialties
Rotisserie Oven Cooking
The Sandwich Maker Cookbook
The Sensational Skillet: Sautés and
   Stir-Fries
Slow Cooking in Crock-Pot,® Slow
   Cooker, Oven and Multi-Cooker
Soups and Stews
The Toaster Oven Cookbook
Unbeatable Chicken Recipes
The Vegetarian Slow Cooker
New Waffles and Pizzelles
The Well Dressed Potato
Wraps and Roll-Ups

For a free catalog, call: Bristol Publishing Enterprises, Inc.
(800) 346-4889
www.bristolcookbooks.com